Department of Social Security
Information and Library Services

Room 114, Adelphi
1-11 John Adam Street

Best Practice

IS PRACTICE GUIDES

IS strategy: process and products

FORMAT
PUBLISHING

First published 1999

ISBN 1 903091 00 4

For information about the availability of CCTA's
IS Management and IS Practice guides, contact:

Central Computer and Telecommunications Agency
Rosebery Court   Steel House
St Andrews Business Park   Tothill Street
Norwich NR7 0HS   London SW1H 9NF

Telephone   +44 (0) 1603 704567
Email   info@ccta.gsi.gov.uk
Website   www.ccta.gov.uk

This book is published by:

Format Publishing Limited
9-10 Redwell Street
Norwich
Norfolk NR2 4SN

Telephone   +44 (0) 1603 766544
Email   info@formatpublishing.co.uk
Website   www.formatpublishing.co.uk

Edited, designed and typeset by Format Information Design.

Printed in the UK.

Contents

CONTENTS

CHAPTER ONE
Introduction

1.1 Purpose of this guide

Every public sector organisation needs a strategy to manage its business information. This guide is intended to help public sector organisations to formulate an IS strategy as an integral part of thinking strategically about the business, its information requirements and processes – all of this in times of radical change. It is essential to think strategically about how information systems (IS) can enable business change.

An IS strategy sets out the long-term role that information systems will play in the support and development of the organisation's business, and the way in which information systems will be managed for the benefit of the business. The IS strategy is the concern of business management; it is distinguished from the information technology (IT) strategy, which is primarily the concern of internal or external service providers.

This guide explains how to:
- conduct an IS strategy study where this is part of an organisation's formulation of IS strategy
- achieve effective progression of the strategy – an ongoing activity beyond strategy formulation.

Most organisations will already have an IS strategy. The guidance in this volume is intended to help with a strategy review as well as the formulation of a new strategy; the same basic principles apply for both.

The companion volume *Strategic Management of Information Systems* positions the IS strategy in the context of strategic decisions and management action.

1.2 The outcome for the organisation

This guide presents an approach to the development or review of an IS strategy and suggests the deliverables which will be produced from the development activity. It should be understood that the IS strategy study and the outputs from it are intermediate goals. They are only steps along the way to the achievement of the desired outcome for the organisation: the strategic management of its information systems. The characteristics of strategic management for IS are:
- the ability to develop capabilities to deal with a vaguely defined future
- the ability to invest effectively in infrastructure and systems projects
- the integration of IS strategy with the wider business strategy of the organisation

- the recognition that senior business management are responsible for, and must be involved in, the formulation of the IS strategy and the continuous progression and monitoring of the strategy
- the recognition of the distinction between the IS strategy and the supporting IT strategy, and the respective responsibilities for the two strategies
- a distinguishing of the IS strategy from the low-level implementation plans for projects and programmes, while ensuring that these contribute to the realisation of the strategy
- the identification of key areas of concern for business management in relation to the organisation's information systems, in the form of the strategic themes of the IS strategy
- the maintenance and effective operation of organisational structures, policies, roles and responsibilities which support the strategic management of information systems
- the proactive role of business management in the deployment of information systems for business benefit and for effecting and supporting business change, including changes in its interactions with the business environment
- the ability of the organisation to learn from its experience in managing information systems, and to identify opportunities for continuous improvement in its IS and business operations.

The approach set out in Part B will assist the organisation in moving towards the exercise of strategic management of its information systems, through the changes arising from the recommendations of the IS strategy study and documented in the strategy statement. The approach is not prescriptive; it would be counter-productive to follow the sequence of activities described there unthinkingly. For example, in some circumstances the organisation may be able to formulate the IS strategy and identify the strategic themes through intensive interactive sessions with senior management, or by exploiting previous work undertaken on Public Service Agreements (PSAs) or Business Plans. PSAs set out the planned outputs and outcomes for central government departments and agencies, and the IS strategy is one means of delivering these. Each organisation should find its own route to Strategic Management of IS, compatible with its business operations and management culture. This guide will help those organisations wanting some indication of where to start and how to proceed.

When the organisation has achieved the desired outcome, and displays the characteristics of strategic management as outlined earlier, it may not need to undertake any further full-scale strategy studies. As described in Chapter 10, *Progressing the IS strategy,* the IS strategy will be maintained, monitored and updated as part of the standard business management processes. However, a major review of the strategy may be required in response to significant developments within the organisation, or in its business environment, and an annual review should be conducted to ensure that the IS strategy is still relevant and complete. In all cases, the active participation of senior business management is essential for success.

The approaches described in this guide should be appropriate for most organisations, and can be adapted for large-scale or complex studies.

1.3 Why think strategically about IS?

Why should information and information systems be seen as a strategic business issue?

Information is critical for every business, whether in the public or private sector. Most public sector organisations now depend upon information systems and the IT that supports them. Some public sector bodies, such as those engaged primarily in policy work, deal almost exclusively with information in one form or another. For most organisations, it is essential to formulate a strategy which will ensure the most effective contribution of information systems to the business. IS can greatly improve effectiveness and efficiency; provided the organisation thinks strategically about its information and information systems, they can open up new business opportunities and new ways of doing things.

In today's business environment, there will be periods of major change, often change that cannot be forecast; thus current approaches to strategic thinking must provide robust results to cope with uncertainty. The IS strategy:
- helps to ensure that IS/IT is integrated with the business strategy and supports the business, whatever the changes ahead
- provides a clarity of purpose, common understanding and a framework for detailed planning
- gives the organisation a focus on the strategic developments it should be pursuing and a view of the future towards which it is moving.

In summary, the benefits of a formal IS strategy include:
- clarity of purpose
- common understanding
- a framework for detailed planning
- a description of the desired future
- an indication of the direction of change.

The IS strategy sets out the agenda for change in the organisation's information systems. It is an integral part of the business strategy and corporate change management. It contributes to, and is influenced by, business process redesign exercises, efficiency/value for money activities and the Human Resources (HR) strategy. In addition, it is a major contributor to changes in work practices and procedures for external communications. Its scope can include all the information-handling roles in the organisation, including the Library and the Registry.

There is no universal strategy for all situations. An IS strategy addresses the different requirements of business functions, such as policy units, operations or support/administration functions. There are also different organisational characteristics to take into account, such as federal or centralised control and the maturity of the organisation's deployment of IS/IT. In addition, there may be shared strategies where organisations are working together.

1.4 IS as part of business change

The IS strategy should be seen in the context of the wider business strategy of the organisation. Changes and developments in information systems should be seen as elements in the programmes of business change undertaken by the organisation in response to the challenges and opportunities confronting it. The IS strategy will identify IS-related initiatives which will need to be pursued in parallel with, and integrated with, developments in other functional and support areas of the organisation. For example, as part of its business strategy an organisation may be moving towards electronic delivery of its services. The programme that is established to bring about this change will involve changes in:

- IT infrastructure
- IS and business applications
- staffing, roles and responsibilities in the organisation
- 'front-office' functions
- business processes.

Potentially, there will be changes in the nature of the services themselves – in the scope of the services delivered and the responsibilities shared between the public and private sector for service delivery. At a certain point, the organisation will initiate IS specific and IT specific projects, but it should be recognised that this is part of a wider initiative that has to be managed as a programme. Some IS/IT projects, such as those concerned with technical and information infrastructure, may be managed by the in-house IT unit or external service providers. But where IS/IT elements are contributing to a programme of business change, the business takes ultimate responsibility for the programme.

A strategic requirement for change, such as the widespread introduction of electronic service delivery, can be regarded as a *strategic theme* for IS development – that is, something that the organisation must address if it is to meet its strategic business objectives. More generally, the IS strategy will be based on the definition of a small number of themes which define the context for managing change and dealing with uncertainty – with a focus on the desired direction for the business in pursuit of its objectives, rather than on detailed plans for a fixed planning horizon.

1.5 Strategic themes

A theme will be a significant topic, related to strategic change, which is of concern to the business management of the organisation. It is a topic which the business management will wish to keep under review for the foreseeable future, as part of the task of monitoring the performance of the business and the achievement of its business objectives. A theme which appears in the IS strategy will necessarily be focused on IS/IT-related developments. But most themes will also require developments and changes in other areas of the organisation. A theme will recognise the other dimensions of change required to realise the strategy, such as changes in organisation, business processes, responsibilities, working methods and procedures, management and technical policies, administrative support, external relationships and so on.

1.6 Relationship between the business, IS, IT and organisation, management and policies

In developing the IS strategy, you will need to distinguish the information-based services delivered to users from the technology which supports the service delivery. This distinction is expressed in terms of:

- *IS (Information Systems)* – the combination of computer-based business applications, data, human activities and information-handling procedures which utilise IT components to deliver information services to users in the organisation and possibly outside it. Requirements for information systems are defined by the business of the organisation – the IS strategy for the organisation is business-focused

- *IT (Information Technology)* – the underlying hardware, software and communications infrastructure; the platforms, components, common facilities and technology framework on which the delivery of information services is based. The design, development and operation of the technical infrastructure are the concern of technology and IS/IT service providers, who may be internal to the organisation or external suppliers. The IT strategy for the organisation is technology focused.

Figure 1 shows the relationships between IS, IT and organisation, management and policies. The IS strategy should be seen as a constituent part of the wider business strategy; the three components will be consistent with relevant aspects of the business strategy of the organisation.

The IS strategy for the organisation is the responsibility of the business management. The IT strategy is the responsibility of technical management, although responsibility for some or all of the IT strategy may be assigned to external contractors and service providers.

IS strategy

The business has requirements for information handling which are addressed by the *IS strategy*. The scope of the IS strategy depends on the role of information in the business unit; it will normally take into account:

- the information-handling requirements of the business functions and different categories of users
- the logical IS architecture to support information handling
- communications and information flows

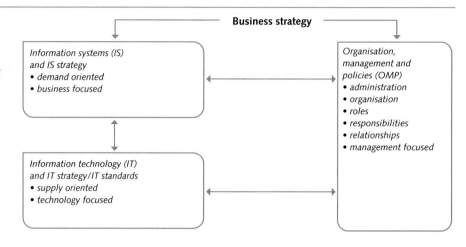

Figure 1:
Relationship between the
business, IS, IT and
organisation, management
and policies

- requirements for business applications
- requirements for management information
- the use of information systems to develop and transform the business.

IT strategy

The role of the *IT strategy* is primarily to provide a technological underpinning to satisfying the business-led requirements of the IS strategy. However, the direction of influence is not one-way: the IT strategy and the provider organisation may suggest technology developments which could benefit the business and feed into the IS strategy. Information technology is concerned with:

- technical standards and interfaces
- interoperability
- technology platforms
- physical architecture
- hardware and software infrastructure
- application development
- system integration of technology
- communications networks.

Organisation, management
and policies

Both the business (IS) and the provider (IT) need to be managed, and the relationship between them must be defined. This is the purpose of organisation, management and policies (OMP) – which constitutes the third major area of concern of the IS strategy. Often referred to as *governance*, it sets out the roles and responsibilities for management of IS in the organisation, including oversight of the IS strategy, and the policies and procedures which will apply to the business exploitation of information systems. Where the provider is wholly or partly in-house, for example, in an internal IT unit, the organisation and responsibilities of the unit will be defined. Whether the provider is in-house or external, the IS strategy will set out the policies and procedures for ensuring that the requirements of the business for IS/IT products and services are satisfied. Organisation, management and policies cover:

- business and provider organisation, management and policies
- business/provider relationships
- roles and responsibilities
- progression of strategies for IS and IT
- management and technical policies
- financing IS/IT – budgeting, charging
- sourcing, procurement.

OMP statements could be part of the strategy statement or issued as a separate, complementary document. The development of the IS strategy and IT strategy are normally separate activities. This guidance is concerned primarily with the development of the IS strategy. CCTA's IT Infrastructure Library (ITIL) provides detailed guidance on IT strategy and infrastructure issues.

1.7 Who is involved in strategy formulation?

Business managers and their advisers on IS/IT, where appropriate, must work closely with the team formulating the strategy. The business, as demanders, must be in control, not the providers of IS/IT. It is essential for business managers and top management to be actively involved – a goal that is often difficult to achieve but fundamental to success.

Business managers often assume that 'information' is an IT issue and of concern only to the technology suppliers. It is vital for the business to recognise that while IT, as a provider issue, can be delegated to the IT unit or external suppliers, IS is a business issue. Senior managers need to recognise that IS cannot be devolved to support functions in the same way as HR and Finance. IS is different because of the degree of dependence it generates, the pace of change, the complexity and the enormous spend.

1.8 Partnerships

Many organisations are now working together in partnership with others in the public sector – for example, central and local government are collaborating to deliver services to the citizen. The basic principles of strategy formulation will apply; consensus across the partnership on shared policies, systems and infrastructure will be key components of the strategy.

1.9 Target audience for this guide

The target audience for this guide includes:

- business managers and their advisers on IS/IT (including the Intelligent Customer function or equivalent, where appropriate); they need to be aware of the IS strategy contributions to business outcomes, and the requirement for the business to be actively involved in setting the strategic direction and progressing the strategic themes

- staff responsible for developing and reviewing the IS strategy; they will need to know about strategy formulation – what to do and how to do it
- in-house IT Directorates as providers of IS/IT services, and in their dealings with external suppliers and service providers
- the IS services industry; they will need to have an understanding of what will be expected of them as consultants advising on strategy study teams and/or as providers of services.

1.10 The research for this guidance

The guidance has been developed from extensive research into current thinking and practice in both the public and private sectors, drawing on published papers and interviews/studies with a number of leading organisations involved in major change. It also builds on established best practice, including CCTA's IS Guide *A2: Strategic Planning for Information Systems*, as feedback reveals that many of the principles in that guidance are timeless. This guidance responds to lessons learned and the experiences of real-world practical issues, as reported by consultants in CCTA's Strategic Assignments Consultancy Service and their clients. In addition, it incorporates the comments of contributors to CCTA workshops and other review channels. These contributions are acknowledged with thanks.

PART A
Principles

CHAPTER TWO

Overview: the IS strategy and its formulation

This chapter outlines the key principles of the new approach to IS strategy formulation, taking into account today's business environment and the need to cope with change.

2.1 Requirements for today's IS strategies

All organisations must be able to cope with change, both internal and in their business environment. Today, the pace of change appears to be accelerating, particularly in the development of information technologies and their application to the business. Any business strategy, including an IS strategy, must be flexible enough to accommodate the demands of continuous change. This means that the IS strategy should be concerned less with a focus on a predetermined desired end-point – which could rapidly prove to be unattainable or irrelevant – and more with the ability to adapt to changing circumstances. The IS strategy should be expressed as a framework of strategic *themes* which define the critical areas of achievement for the business and their desired outcomes, while allowing the business to adapt its detailed plans – the route to the outcomes – in the light of the changing business environment.

In addition, most IS strategies now have a wider scope than before, looking beyond organisational boundaries. IS strategies are no longer self-contained within an organisation, because most organisations are now part of much wider networks of partners, providers and customers. They may be sharing information and transacting business by electronic commerce. Central initiatives require closer integration of public sector bodies (central and local government) and breaking down barriers between organisations. Today's IS strategies must take into account this trend, with the associated implications for information exchange, security and so on.

Strategic thinking

Formulating an IS strategy, or any strategy, should not be regarded as a mechanistic task which can be undertaken according to a rigid formula. Development of a strategy is a creative activity, requiring skills often described as 'strategic thinking'. The characteristics of strategic thinking can be summarised as:

- *an ability to see the 'whole picture'* – the IS strategy will affect all parts of the organisation and its business, and its relationships with organisations in its environment. The development of the IS strategy requires the ability to look across all aspects of the organisation and understand the connections between them, both now and in various possible futures
- *creativity* – the IS strategy will be an agenda for change in the organisation, and the development of the IS strategy defines the desirable future for the business and the direction to take towards it. Strategic thinking is 'divergent' – it

involves the creation of new possibilities, and assessing options which may not have been considered previously. It requires the ability to think outside existing boundaries and constraints

- *scenario generation and evaluation* – the development of an IS strategy will involve consideration of many possible 'futures' for the organisation and its information systems. These futures – or scenarios – must be envisaged by the strategy team and evaluated in terms of the likely impact of developments within and outside the organisation. Strategic thinking involves the ability to formulate and respond to "What if …?" questions
- *ability to deal with ambiguity and uncertainty* – the development of an IS strategy will throw up many questions, not all of which will have answers in the short term, if at all. The strategy team must be prepared to deal with a mass of information which will be incomplete and sometimes conflicting; it must be able to pick out the important messages hidden in the information and to structure them in a way that will be meaningful to the business
- *identification of strategic issues* – the strategy will be driven by the team's perception of the challenges and opportunities facing the organisation (the issues), and its strategic response to them (the strategic themes). Identifying the strategic issues which will be important to the organisation in the longer term is critical to strategic thinking (see section 3.1).

Strategic thinking is not the same as planning. The main characteristic of the planning activity is *analysis*: starting with a defined objective, or output, and generating increasingly detailed breakdowns of the activities and resources required to meet the objectives. The main characteristic of strategy formulation in the early stages of the IS strategy study is *synthesis*: identifying patterns and creating possibilities from a wide spectrum of inputs. The latter part of the IS strategy study involves moving from strategy formulation to high level planning, as the basis for more detailed planning and implementation. So, the focus of the strategy study gradually changes from synthesis, creativity and divergent thinking to analysis, quantification and convergent thinking.

The companion volume *Techniques* describes various approaches to creativity and divergent thinking.

2.2 The approach

The IS strategy today is about process, themes/issues and a progression towards required outcomes. It is more concerned with learning how to deal with change and uncertainty than with setting out a detailed 'road-map' towards a defined future target. Earlier IS strategies assumed a stable business environment, with a fixed planning horizon of around five to ten years. This approach was not always successful, as the business environment of the public sector is never static. In today's climate of radical change, it is said that the only certainty is uncertainty. But without some direction to work towards, there are real risks of lost

Figure 2:
The IS strategy cycle

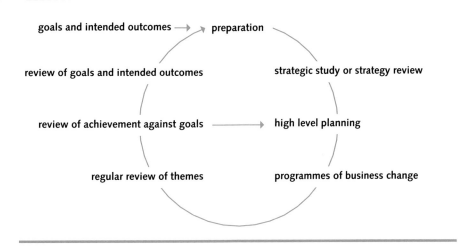

opportunities, expensive mistakes and failure to achieve business objectives. The solution is to identify the strategic issues confronting the organisation and then to develop the strategy as a coherent set of strategic themes that make up a 'big picture' of the organisation's direction. The strategic themes are addressed through interrelated programmes of business change. When goalposts move, the strategic themes still continue to facilitate business change; they can be updated, refocused and changed as necessary, to provide a revised context for the review and updating of detailed plans.

Strategy cycle

The IS strategy cycle is made up of the following stage, as shown in Figure 2:
- *preparation* – planning and scoping
- *strategy study or strategy review* – radical thinking; identification of strategic themes and strategy definition
- *high level planning* – identifying candidates for action
- *programmes of business change* – which include non-strategic IS/IT
- *regular review of the strategic themes* – with a direct link across the cycle to changes in high level planning
- review of goals and intended outcomes, leading to new study.

Components of the
IS strategy

The strategy is separated from detailed plans. It is made up of:
- a strategy statement describing the themes
- a list of candidates for action ('shopping list' for implementation)
- a high level plan – profiles for action made up of selections from the 'shopping list'.

Detailed plans, schedules and resource costings will be produced for the implementation profiles. Rolled into this will be the implementation plans for other IS/IT projects and activities. A 'road map' is a useful product of the high level planning process. Its content is flexible, acknowledging that plans will probably change over time. Its purpose is to show how non-strategic IS developments fit into the plan, their expected lifetime and how they are eventually brought back onto the strategic path.

2.3 Summary

In summary, the characteristics of the new approach to strategy formulation are:
- outcome driven
- a fast-track approach to the strategy study
- a business focus – because the business depends on information
- strategic themes as stepping stones between where we are now and where we want to be
- a strategic agenda for change
- management visibility
- separating the IS strategy from the detailed planning – it is about progressing the strategy and implementing plans. The IS strategy as a set of themes is not a finite programme and thus cannot be costed, but organisations will want to cost the plans as far as possible with estimates
- above all, *strategic thinking* – an ability and a willingness to think strategically about the agenda for change, with perhaps a new and radically different direction.

At the conclusion of the strategy formulation, there is an interface to Programme Management. But the IS strategy is not static. It is kept under constant review through the progression of the strategic themes.

Critical success factors for the study are:
- there must be continuous involvement of business management from the outset
- where strategic partners are involved in IS/IT service delivery, there must be a shared understanding of the benefits to be derived from the combined IS and IT strategies
- there must be a willingness to think strategically, and receptiveness to new ideas
- throughout the strategy study there must be evaluation of the potential for IS/IT to enable change (for example, providing new opportunities for service delivery) – or to block progress (for example, existing infrastructure that cannot be enhanced cost-effectively).

CHAPTER THREE

Strategic issues and strategic themes

This chapter explains the principles of strategic issues and strategic themes, the recommended approach for developing an IS strategy and progressing it through uncertainty and change. In summary:

- an issue is a challenge facing the organisation (problem or opportunity)
- the themes of the IS strategy between them embody responses to the issues, where there is an identifiable IS/IT dimension to the response.

3.1 Strategic issues

There is not necessarily a one-to-one relationship between the issues and the themes. Some business issues will have no IS/IT dimension in their responses; some IS themes may address aspects of several issues.

The IS strategy aims to address those topics which are of concern to both the organisation as a whole and its senior management. Such topics will include the issues which confront the organisation. An *issue* is a challenge facing the organisation which must be addressed: it may be represented as a problem or an opportunity. Successfully addressing a business issue can be thought of as a key success factor for the business strategy. In the *Information gathering* stage of the IS strategy study, the team will be concerned to identify the business-related and IS-related issues facing the organisation, and to identify those issues which can be addressed with IS/IT support (the response to some issues will lie outside the scope of the IS strategy).

There is no single set of issues to which every organisation must respond. The range of relevant issues will depend on individual circumstances, although many organisations will identify common concerns.

3.2 The IS/IT dimension: strategic themes

The IS strategy statement will set out a high level view of the direction which the organisation wishes to take for IS/IT, based on service delivery and definition, the development and management of its information systems and their deployment in support of the business. The statement of direction can be expressed in terms of the realisation of a small number of strategic *themes* which between them encompass the most critical areas of achievement for the IS strategy. The themes for the IS strategy will, between them, respond to the issues facing the organisation, where those issues have an IS/IT dimension.

Themes in the IS strategy can be regarded as the 'strategy success factors' – the things which the organisation must get right if the business is to derive the maximum benefit from the potential of IS/IT. They are the areas of IS/IT-related development and change which will make the most important contributions to supporting or promoting the business, management or organisational changes and improvements sought by the organisation over the next few years. A theme is an IS/IT-related grouping of developments and other changes which will help to take the organisation forward in pursuit of its business strategy and objectives. In IS terms, the themes should, between them, cover all the applications designated *strategic* in the categorisation of applications documented in the IS strategy study.

A theme in the IS strategy will necessarily be focused on IS/IT-related developments, but will recognise the other dimensions of change required to realise the strategy, such as changes in organisation, business processes, responsibilities, working methods and procedures, management and technical policies, administrative support, external relationships and so on. A theme will, therefore, not be concerned solely with software application developments, and the developments identified for each theme will need to look beyond the confines of IS/IT for their realisation.

3.3 Implementing strategic themes

The senior management of the organisation will not wish to be involved in monitoring the progress of large numbers of individual projects; they will be able to maintain a high level focus on the development and achievement of the IS strategy by monitoring the progress in each of the themes. For the purposes of detailed planning and implementation, however, it will be necessary to break down each theme into a number of implementation areas.

Figure 3 shows the relationship between strategic issues, strategic themes and programmes of business change.

It will be possible to suggest a potentially large number of *candidates for action*, each of which could be established as a discrete project. A candidate for action could be, for example, an application or infrastructure development, a feasibility study, the development of policies for IS/IT, or a change in organisational arrangements for IS/IT. The list of candidate activities is used as input to the detailed implementation planning, which selects and prioritises a shortlisted portfolio of the activities to be implemented over the next planning period – for example, 12-24 months. Different portfolios of developments will produce different profiles of programmes of change and will have different profiles of costs and benefits associated with them. Those activities which are not selected are maintained on the candidate list for consideration in the next cycle of detailed implementation planning.

The planning of individual developments or projects will normally be undertaken as part of a wider plan of business change, in which the IS/IT component is integrated with other activities in the business plan. Technical developments which are not owned by a single business area, such as IS/IT infrastructure projects, will be planned centrally by the IT unit or an external supplier.

Figure 3:
Strategic issues and
programmes of
business change

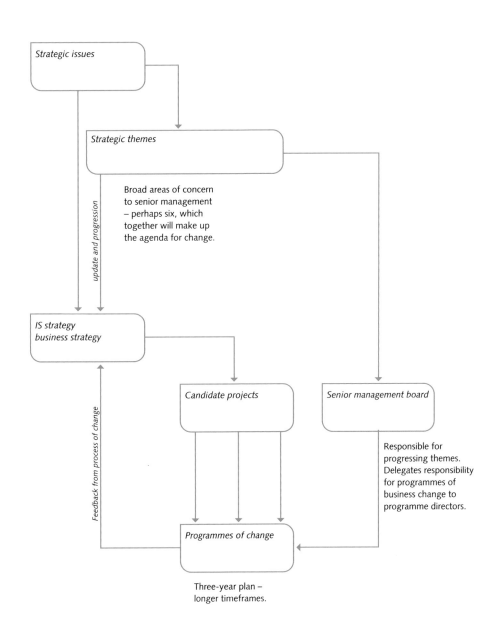

The themes should be regarded as overlapping and interrelated rather than distinct self-contained programmes. Progress in realising the IS vision for the organisation will be achieved through the implementation of action plans whose scope, timing and content will be subject to detailed planning as part of the implementation of the IS/IT development portfolio. An individual development project may contribute to one or more of the themes; and some development projects, while of importance to particular areas of the organisation, will not necessarily make a major contribution to any of the themes supporting the corporate IS strategy.

To illustrate the relationship between strategic issues, strategic themes and candidates for action, an example for a policy unit might be:
- *strategic issue* – the pressure to improve support to ministerial decision-making in the context of joined-up government
- *strategic theme* – improvements in information provision and dissemination within the business unit
- *candidates for action* – might include Electronic Document Management, Electronic Record Management, internet access and review of library services.

3.4 Non-strategic IS/IT

In order for the IS/IT providers to have a complete view of the requirements for IS/IT support and development, the organisation must look more widely than 'strategic' applications and must also consider current and future IS/IT-related developments which can be regarded as necessary or useful, but not strategic (see *Provider considerations* in section 9.3). Typically, these developments will address or anticipate problems with current systems, or help to maintain the smooth operation of the business, but will not take the business forward into new areas, significant improvements in efficiency or effectiveness, or changed ways of working. They may include developments needed to satisfy new statutory requirements, non-discretionary developments, development of applications which do not make a significant organisation-wide contribution to business objectives, ongoing maintenance and support of existing facilities and upgrades needed to replace obsolete technology.

Where the response to these requirements raises strategic issues, it should be addressed in the IS strategy or IT strategy. For example, the question "What do we do about future support of legacy applications?" can be regarded as raising strategic questions for management, even though the applications themselves have no strategic role.

All of these non-strategic developments and other calls on resources should be addressed in parallel with strategic developments proposed within the themes, and should be prioritised within the same planning and management framework.

3.5 Progressing the themes

The programmes of business change should be implemented through a formal *Programme Management* approach, which will ensure that the objectives of the themes are never obscured by the complexity of the business change. In large organisations, consideration should be given to the appointment of a coordinator for each of the themes. Such a role would encompass responsibility for ensuring that progress was maintained on all of the designated strategies and individual developments scheduled within that theme. Each coordinator would report regularly to the organisation management on the progress of the theme and on any problems which need to be addressed by the senior business management, such as policy, coordination of projects, internal organisation and external relations. The coordinator would need to maintain regular liaison with the individual Programme and Project Managers responsible for the developments contributing to each theme.

The CCTA publication *Managing Successful Programmes* provides detailed guidance.

CHAPTER FOUR

Different types of strategy study

IS strategies and their formulation will take different forms depending on the needs of the organisation. The basic principles will be the same – that is, the identification of strategic issues, development of strategic themes and translation into candidates for action that will contribute to programmes of business change. But the scope will be different for each; the range of strategic issues that could affect the business will be different in each case and the scale of the exercise will vary. This chapter outlines the variables that typically affect the approach to strategy formulation.

4.1 Factors that affect the approach to the IS strategy

Organisations differ widely across the public sector in their scope, business function and relationships with other organisations. These factors will affect the approach to strategy formulation:

- the size of the organisation
- how decisions are taken – ranging from complete decentralisation to collegiate consensus
- the organisation's maturity in its use of IS
- the organisation's structure – for example:
    - monolithic, where business and IS strategy are centralised, versus federal, where business units are small and diverse, but core infrastructure needs are paramount
    - centrally situated – that is, core departments, where the organisation dictates most of the terms with its partners
    - 'virtual' organisations, where there are several organisations, some locally accountable, and a number of Cabinet posts are involved. There will be a need for an overarching infrastructure.

In addition, many organisations are working in partnership and require a shared IS strategy. Outsourcing is a core strategic issue that will be addressed in the IS strategy. In many cases, the responsibility for IT now lies largely outside the organisation (but it is important to note that *responsibility for IS is not outsourced*). This trend is expected to continue as organisations take the decision to form partnerships with IT providers. Responsibilities for IS strategies in a public/private partnership context may require new approaches where some strategic decisions and responsibilities are shared. There may be further complexities to consider where a number of organisations collaborate in the delivery of services.

4.2 Scoping different types of strategy

The starting point is usually to assume an organisation-wide IS strategy. But in a large or complex organisation, you may wish to limit the scope of the strategy to certain aspects of the organisation's business. Similarly, if your organisation has little experience of business or strategic planning, it may be sensible to work towards an organisation-wide view over a period of successive planning cycles, limiting the first strategic plans to clearly defined areas and identifying links with other areas.

Where there is a requirement to work with others across organisational boundaries, electronic service delivery will require access and provision of information across organisations. The requirement may well encompass infrastructure; the broader scope of overarching IT infrastructure is becoming the rule, not the exception. Increasingly, a single strategic IT infrastructure will cover many units, each with distinct business aims and objectives, business and IS strategies. Examples are the Government Secure Intranet (GSI), connecting central government departments and agencies, and NHSnet, which links NHS Trusts and primary care providers, such as GP group practices.

What should the strategy cover?

If your organisation has a single cohesive business, you will probably recommend a single IS strategy. At the other extreme, if your organisation's activities are diverse, a single strategy may be inappropriate because it would fail to accommodate the differing business needs, structures, or cultures. Separate strategies may be realistic where:

- the organisation has separate major business units that bear little relationship to each other in business terms
- those business units have little need to share or exchange information
- different business units do not have to compete for limited IS resources
- the information systems requirements of the individual business units are sufficiently different to make it impractical to devise an organisation-wide strategy to justify investment in infrastructure – but there may be a risk that overall economies of scale could be lost.

One strategy or several?

If you opt for the several-strategy approach, you may also need to consider recommending a high level organisation-wide strategy to give a framework within which the individual strategies can be developed. This corporate strategy can cover issues which cross the boundaries of the individual business units (for example, corporate policy issues, common services, or management information needs).

How many studies?

The preparation stage of strategy formulation (described in Chapter 6, *Preparation*) will determine how many strategy studies are required and the business areas they should cover.

In very large or complex organisations, a number of studies may need to be undertaken. By breaking down the study work into smaller components, it is possible to ensure manageable and achievable progress towards an integrated strategy, avoiding the practical problems of undertaking single, excessively large studies.

Other projects (which are actually studies) might be proposed to investigate specific issues arising within any of the domains of IS, IT or organisation, management and policies (for example, organisational policy for information management).

An advantage of this multi-study approach is that the work can be carried out over different time periods. The most important strategic issues can be addressed first by the higher level studies; the lower level studies can then proceed at a pace which reflects the priorities of the business and the capacity to absorb change.

In large organisations, splitting and phasing study activity is the norm; but beware a massive, bureaucratic planning structure. A number of studies, each with well-defined scope and short duration, normally achieves more than a single, very large study.

There are three commonly used approaches:
- *single IS strategy, single study* – this is the normal approach for small organisations, or organisations that perform relatively homogeneous business functions
- *single IS strategy, multiple studies* – this is the arrangement most commonly adopted in large and complex organisations, where the use of several studies offers more flexibility, and delivers benefits faster, but retains the advantages of a single integrated strategy
- *multiple IS strategies, multiple studies* – this path is normally followed in the case of large, federally structured organisations that embrace separate businesses.

In addition, there may be a requirement for infrastructure strategies and/or a shared strategy where several partners are collaborating on service delivery.

B

PART B
Process

CHAPTER FIVE

The strategy study: getting started

This chapter provides a summary of the stages of the strategy study, together with brief guidance on conducting the study:

- who is involved, their roles and responsibilities
- management of the study as a formal project
- the communication plan
- quality procedures.

5.1 Overview

Information systems and the IS strategy should always be considered within the context of the business and its objectives. The relationship between business strategy and the IS strategy is two-way. All businesses, and particularly public sector organisations, depend on flows of information within and outside the organisation, and on facilities for creating, maintaining, communicating and manipulating information. The business requirements for information handling will, therefore, feed into the IS strategy, and to the underlying strategy for information technology implementation. Conversely, the potential of new information technologies, and the information systems which they make possible, will contribute to business thinking. The availability of technologies such as the internet, electronic commerce and smart cards, suggests new ways of conducting business, and even new business areas for exploitation. Work on the IS strategy should be integrated with the development of the business strategy, since the two are closely connected. It is not sufficient to 'align' the IS strategy with a pre-defined business strategy – they should be developed in tandem. Programmes of business change can then be planned in concert with the developments in IS/IT needed to support them. Where there is no clear business strategy, the IS strategy study will need to place more emphasis on business anaysis (see section 6.4).

The approach to strategy formulation

As stated in Chapter 1, *Introduction*, the study (or the report it produces) is not the strategy. Only when high level decisions and actions actually reflect and embody consistent principles will there be a strategy to point to. The study can suggest, articulate, or inform the development of such principles.

The process outlined in this chapter is intended to provide a framework for your own decision-making. It is not a prescriptive approach; you should tailor the framework to your organisation's specific requirements. Strategy formulation is a creative process, requiring skills in both analysis and synthesis. You will need to iterate between stages/phases as your thoughts develop. Stages may overlap; the activities within a stage are not sequential and activities in different stages may be interdependent. The important points are that there must be thorough preparation,

Figure 4:
Stages of the strategy study

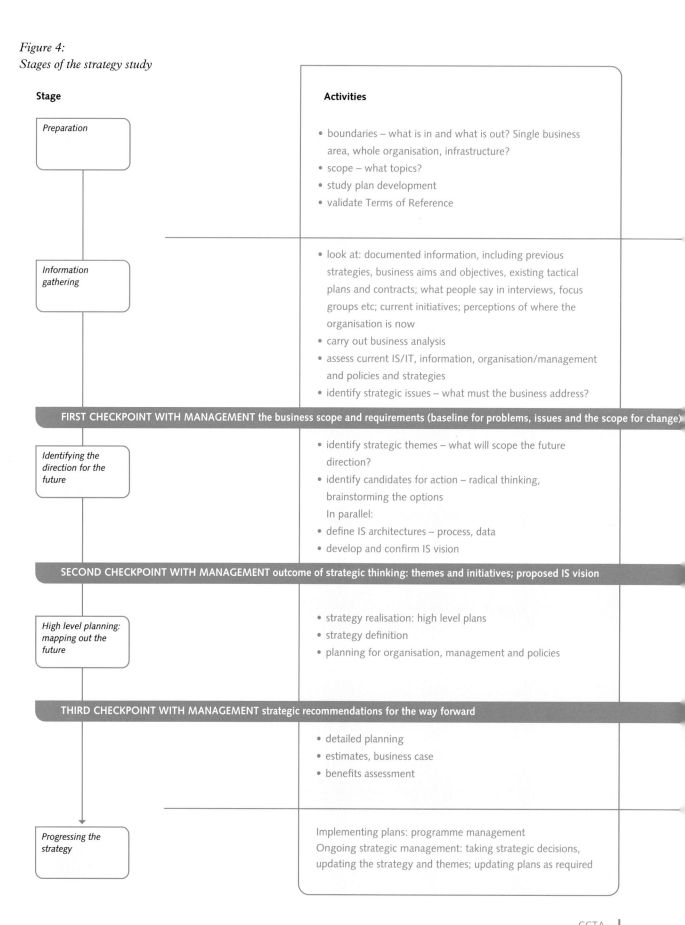

Stage

Activities

Preparation

- boundaries – what is in and what is out? Single business area, whole organisation, infrastructure?
- scope – what topics?
- study plan development
- validate Terms of Reference

Information gathering

- look at: documented information, including previous strategies, business aims and objectives, existing tactical plans and contracts; what people say in interviews, focus groups etc; current initiatives; perceptions of where the organisation is now
- carry out business analysis
- assess current IS/IT, information, organisation/management and policies and strategies
- identify strategic issues – what must the business address?

FIRST CHECKPOINT WITH MANAGEMENT the business scope and requirements (baseline for problems, issues and the scope for change)

Identifying the direction for the future

- identify strategic themes – what will scope the future direction?
- identify candidates for action – radical thinking, brainstorming the options
  In parallel:
- define IS architectures – process, data
- develop and confirm IS vision

SECOND CHECKPOINT WITH MANAGEMENT outcome of strategic thinking: themes and initiatives; proposed IS vision

High level planning: mapping out the future

- strategy realisation: high level plans
- strategy definition
- planning for organisation, management and policies

THIRD CHECKPOINT WITH MANAGEMENT strategic recommendations for the way forward

- detailed planning
- estimates, business case
- benefits assessment

Progressing the strategy

Implementing plans: programme management
Ongoing strategic management: taking strategic decisions, updating the strategy and themes; updating plans as required

Products	**Comments**
• boundaries: organisational view of strategy • initial view of scope: topics to be addressed in strategy • initial view of business environment • preliminary interview list • outline source information list • outline study plan • validated TORs	Essential to have thorough planning – successful outcome of study depends on this Focus on where to find information, who to ask, who to tell, who to confirm
• business drivers, priorities • strategic issues • models of the business • information about processes • assessments of current position, risks and scope for change • assumptions and the business scope	What is possible? *Strategic thinking about the scope for change, following* *Information gathering and analysis: early thinking about strategic issues, opportunities, collaboration with others, partnerships etc* *IS as part of business change, not a separate component*
• definition of themes • candidate projects for each theme • options for implementation • broad architecture and standards • vision statement	Divergent thinking *Radical questions: how can we do things differently?* *In-depth considerations of the need to work together and share information/processes with other organisations in and outside the public sector. Focus on business change: will IS be an enabler or a blocker?* *Addressing the need to cope with uncertainty*
High level plans for action: • strategic, ongoing, other • recommended way forward • strategy statement • plans and policies for organisation, management and policies; sourcing; architecture and IT standards	How? Convergent thinking *High level planning for business change* *Strategy statement separated from plans* *Changes in organisation, management and policies for IS/IT*
• study report • profiles linked to programmes of change • programme definition(s) • business case(s)	Detailed planning

strategic thinking throughout and a readiness to consider radical change. The key to success is to apply the principles of strategic thinking to the needs and circumstances of the organisation.

The role of techniques

There is a wealth of experience available on when and how to carry out the processes relevant to strategy formulation. Techniques embody this experience. The big risk lies in 'doing the technique' rather than developing the strategy. Most experienced analysts who are new to strategy work will go too deep in applying techniques, especially the analytical approaches. Techniques are not a substitute for judgement; guidelines are needed to know when to stop.

Techniques fall into two broad categories – analytic and synthetic. Each category includes a few core techniques, which should always be used, and a much larger body of techniques which can be useful under certain circumstances, but which can be disruptive or wasteful if used inappropriately. Descriptions in the companion volume *Techniques* make these distinctions, and seek to offer guidelines on when the use of a technique is likely to yield a good result.

The stages of the strategy cycle

Figure 4 shows the stages of the strategy study, with an outline of the activities and interim deliverables at each stage, together with a brief commentary on each stage. The stages are:
- preparation
- information gathering
- identifying the future direction
- high level planning
- progressing the strategy.

5.2 Who is involved

The people involved in strategy formulation are senior management, the study team and the wider organisation (business managers, end users of IS/IT and others with a stake in the successful outcome of the strategy, including service partners). The interests and concerns of the wider organisation will be addressed during the study through focus groups, interviews and awareness briefings. The roles and responsibilities of both management and the study team are described below.

Senior management

There must be senior management involvement, with the following roles clearly identified:
- a 'champion' for the strategy
- beneficiaries who will gain from the strategy's implementation
- 'deliverers' – those who deliver the benefits from programmes of business change.

The main concerns of management in relation to the IS strategy study are:
- to ensure that the work of the study team is properly directed

- to ensure that the evolving IS strategy is directly harnessed to business and policy objectives and priorities
- to review and approve the progress of the study at designated checkpoints, and to approve the continuation of the study to the next stage
- to approve the formal deliverables of the study.

Subsequently, management's concerns will be:
- to ensure that implementation plans for business change are carried through
- to progress the strategy through strategic themes
- to ensure that benefits are delivered and objectives met
- to ensure continuing compliance with business priorities.

Strategy study team

For smaller organisations, study team members will probably contribute on a part-time basis and individual team members may take several roles. In larger organisations there may be a full-time team with additional members coopted from time to time.

The study team can consist of both internal staff and external consultants. Staff who were involved in the *Preparation* stage may be involved in the subsequent stages, particularly if they have business analysis skills. IS/IT specialists should also be involved; it is essential to represent a provider view and provide input on the business potential of technology.

The precise composition of the team will vary according to the nature and scope of the study and the degree of in-house expertise and experience available. The composition of the team will also vary depending on what stage the study has reached. In the key stages of *information gathering* and identifying the direction for the future, the accent is on business and strategic issues. The essential requirement in these phases is for business managers who:
- have the confidence of top management
- can discuss corporate issues with them freely
- have a willingness to consider radical solutions
- are aware of the potential of IT.

Role of consultants

In later stages, as options for information systems solutions are being investigated, understanding of technology issues becomes important. Throughout, the team needs to be led by business-oriented managers who can ensure that the strategic emphasis is retained and continuity of the thinking process maintained.

The development of an IS strategy requires skills and expertise in a variety of disciplines and it is unlikely that all will be available in smaller organisations. Some of the benefits of using consultancy firms are that:
- consultants can suggest approaches, techniques and methods based on

previous experience (particularly useful if you are embarking on an initial strategic study)

- they can advise on the scope, duration, and resource requirements of the strategic planning exercise
- they can assist with management and organisational aspects of the strategy
- they can provide an awareness of technological advances and their potential
- they provide an independent view and may help the organisation's staff to reach a consensus.

5.3 Management of the study as a project

The IS strategy study or review should be managed as a project, with the application of appropriate project management disciplines and procedures: planning, resource management, management of timetable and milestones, specification of deliverables, management of dependencies, internal and external reporting and so on.

It is likely that the study will accumulate a large volume of paper and electronic documentation, collected from external sources and generated by the study team. Even for small-scale studies, members of the study team will be producing documentation which is subject to revision and update, such as working papers or drafts of formal deliverables; formal configuration management procedures should be applied. In this way, all team members will be assured that they have the current version of documents and can trace the development of drafts if necessary.

It is important to keep team members fully briefed and aware of developments. One approach is to have weekly team meetings to keep information updated.

Working papers

Working papers play an important role in the strategy formulation process and form the basis of the strategy statement. Depending on the topic and the scale of the study, these papers may be just a few paragraphs or a number of pages. The production of working papers:

- ensures that all relevant topics are addressed during the study
- provides milestones and checkpoints against which progress can be monitored and quality assured
- assists study team members to structure their exploration of particular topics in the study
- provides a vehicle for staff outside the study team to contribute to the work of strategy formulation
- enables the study team to communicate the early results of work in progress to a wider audience
- helps to maintain the interest and involvement of the business and their ownership of the strategy process
- helps study team members to identify areas of uncertainty where further investigation is required

- generates material which will be carried forward to the formal deliverables of the study
- provides a focus for feedback and interaction with the business.

The production of working papers should be planned as part of the study time-table. Depending on the scale of the study, it may be useful to produce a separate production schedule for working papers, showing their expected production dates and the relationships and dependencies between them.

There is no fixed definitive list of working papers that must be produced. See Chapter 12, *Topics for working papers*.

5.4	**Communication plan**	A communication plan is essential for achieving 'buy-in', ownership and under-standing across the organisation. There should be mechanisms for two-way com-munication. The plan should address who to inform, how to inform them and create an opportunity for the involvement of all staff (including service providers where relevant). Communications should be based on a policy of 'no surprises' so that all staff know what is expected of them and when (see also section 11.5, *Overview of products – communications*).

5.5	**Quality procedures**	An outcome-based approach to quality is the recommended approach; it can be difficult to achieve, but is the only way to ensure fitness for purpose of the strategy.

For the conduct of the study overall, questions which form part of a quality review could include:
- has the consultation process been wide enough?
- were the right people consulted and the right questions asked?
- does the process appear to have been covered adequately (completeness)?
- has a representative range of options and scenarios been considered – and justified in the working papers?
- do the sponsors really feel that they own the strategy?
- have the intractable strategic issues been referred to senior management?

Quality control over the production of working papers can be achieved through the production of a document specification for each paper, where appropriate, and a formal review of the paper against the specification. Working papers will be circulated and comment invited; depending on the study, this may provide all the quality checks that are needed (see Annex C, *Document specification format*, for an example specification).

The production of checklists of topics for interviewers is a valuable tool for ensuring that quality is maintained in the conduct of interviews. Interview reports should be produced to a common format to ensure that comparable information is recorded.

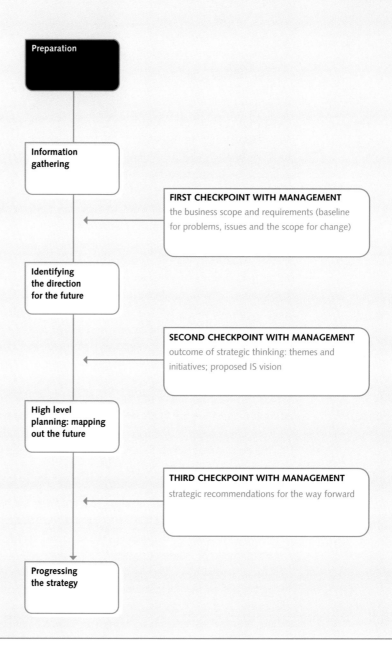

Preparation

Information gathering

FIRST CHECKPOINT WITH MANAGEMENT
the business scope and requirements (baseline
for problems, issues and the scope for change)

**Identifying
the direction
for the future**

SECOND CHECKPOINT WITH MANAGEMENT
outcome of strategic thinking: themes and
initiatives; proposed IS vision

**High level
planning: mapping
out the future**

THIRD CHECKPOINT WITH MANAGEMENT
strategic recommendations for the way forward

**Progressing
the strategy**

Activities
- boundaries – what is in and what is
  out? Single business area, whole
  organisation, infrastructure?
- scope: what topics?
- study plan development
- validate TORs

Products
*Boundaries: organisational extent of
strategy*
*Initial view of scope: topics to be
addressed in strategy*
Initial view of business environment
Preliminary interview list
Outline source information list
Outline study plan
Validated TORs

CHAPTER SIX

Preparation

6.1 Purpose of this stage

The purpose of this stage is to prepare the ground for the detailed study. Thorough preparation is essential: the successful outcome of the study depends on the foundations put in place at the beginning. The objectives of this stage are to ensure that the study team has a sound knowledge of the organisation, its wider environment, and the issues facing it, before detailed work begins. At this initial stage, the study team investigates where to find information, who to interview and/or involve in focus groups, who will have the authority to confirm findings and who to inform as part of the two-way communication process. At the start of this stage, the study team members need to become familiar with the plan for the study, and with the processes and techniques which will be used.

6.2 Boundaries and scope

The *boundaries* are determined: the study team establishes the organisational coverage of the strategy study and the resulting strategy. For example, the requirement may be relatively simple – for an autonomous business unit – or it may be complex – encompassing a number of business areas with shared infrastructure across a number of organisations. There may be a need for a number of strategies. In addition, there may be a need to consider the strategies of partners.

The *scope* is determined: the study team establishes the relationship between the IS strategy study and any previous or current work on the related IT strategy, to determine what is included and what is definitely outside the scope of the IS strategy. Some aspects of information systems in the organisation may be outside the scope of the current study – for example, because they have been the subject of previous detailed studies, the conclusions of which can be taken forward into the current study.

Different types of strategy

What type of strategy will be required? This depends on your organisation and its specific requirements (discussed more fully in Chapter 4, *Different types of strategy studies*).

There are four commonly used approaches:
- single IS strategy, single study
- single IS strategy, multiple studies
- multiple IS strategies, multiple studies
- corporate IS strategy, where several organisations need to share information.

In addition, you may need to consider infrastructure and/or collaborative approaches if your organisation is sharing with others in delivering services.

6.3 Sources of information

The study team needs to gather sufficient information to build an accurate picture of the organisation. This material forms the basis for subsequent phases of the IS strategy study. Sources of information should be identified in the *Preparation* stage, and may include:

- statements or papers on the drivers for change, such as proposed new legislation
- current business plans and any statements of business strategy
- the current IS strategy statement and supporting documents (if these exist)
- business strategy planning documents (if these exist)
- any relevant internal or consultancy reports on key business areas (organisational reviews, efficiency reviews, staff inspection reports)
- any internal papers outlining future policy, or policy options in important business areas
- descriptions of business cycles (budgetary, management accounting, policy evaluation) that will need to be taken into account
- background material on the business of the organisation
- organisation charts and location charts
- statistics illustrating the size and nature of the organisation's expenditure (Public Expenditure Survey, management reports)
- internal or consultancy reports on IS/IT topics
- documentation on existing information systems.

The potential impact of external documents may vary, including:

- external documents that could influence business direction
- external documents that could influence the organisation's management and policies
- external documents that could indicate IS/IT industry direction.

6.4 No corporate plan?

What should you do if there is no corporate plan? The existence of a corporate or business strategy helps greatly in defining a satisfactory IS strategy, but its absence does not make the task impossible.

Where there is no formal corporate or business strategy, the *Preparation* stage will point out the need for the IS strategy study (or studies) to place more emphasis on business analysis, and to determine business objectives in those areas that affect the IS strategy.

Even where some corporate planning work has been undertaken, the study team should proceed cautiously. Such work is often targeted primarily at improving the efficiency and effectiveness of current policy implementation; and although this is a key aim of strategic thinking for IS, future policy issues also have to be addressed by the IS strategy. Often, therefore, the corporate planning work already carried out only forms a platform on which to build the business analysis which the IS strategy requires. The *Preparation* stage should report on the extent to which any corporate planning has addressed the implications of new and emerging business policies and programmes.

6.5 Planning for interviews

In the *Preparation* stage, the study team will identify the interviews to be conducted during the *Information gathering* stage. A small number of key interviews will be needed in the *Preparation* stage – for example, with the sponsors of the IS strategy study, to enable the study team to scope their subsequent work and to confirm management commitment to the study. Interviews with staff in the organisation will be used to:

- obtain information about the business issues, and to discuss how information systems may be of use
- identify explicit and implicit assumptions and initiate the process of challenging them
- gain commitment to the emerging strategy (implementation of the strategy will require the active support of key individuals; even where such individuals may not need to be consulted to obtain information, their commitment may be vital).

Other groups to be interviewed are:

- major customers and suppliers
- business partners – other public sector organisations (such as local government) and the private sector
- strategic partners, such as IS providers
- any key bodies who will have to approve the technical and financial aspects of the IS strategy.

It may be useful to benchmark other public or private sector organisations which conduct similar business activities. You will have the opportunity to learn from their experiences, to see the 'state of the art', and to explore the possibilities for mutual cooperation.

The *initial interview list* developed at this stage will be revised during the *Information gathering* stage.

6.6 Initial view of the business environment

From preliminary *Information gathering* the study team produces an *initial view of the business environment*. This is a narrative description of:

- the organisation's context and relationships – partners, customers and suppliers
- products and services provided by the organisation
- the business elements of the organisation and the issues that face it
- other external areas of constraint or pressure
- basic assumptions regarding the future direction of the organisation
- an initial view of the options and potential for change
- the organisation's business functions and processes
- the organisation's structure and management.

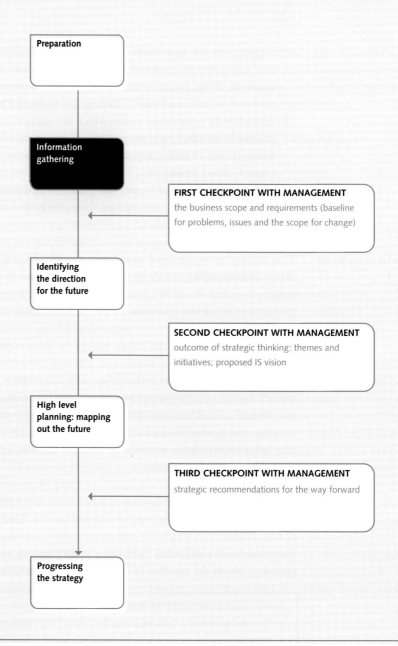

Preparation

Information gathering

FIRST CHECKPOINT WITH MANAGEMENT
the business scope and requirements (baseline for problems, issues and the scope for change)

Identifying the direction for the future

SECOND CHECKPOINT WITH MANAGEMENT
outcome of strategic thinking: themes and initiatives; proposed IS vision

High level planning: mapping out the future

THIRD CHECKPOINT WITH MANAGEMENT
strategic recommendations for the way forward

Progressing the strategy

Activities

- look at: documented information including previous strategies, business aims and objectives, existing tactical plans and contracts; what people say in interviews, focus groups etc; current initiatives; perceptions of where the organisation is now
- carry out business analysis
- assess current IS/IT, information, organisation/management policies and strategies
- identify strategic issues – what must the business address?

Products

Business drivers, priorities
Strategic issues
Models of the business
Information about processes
Assessments of current position, risks and scope for change
Assumptions and the business scope

CHAPTER SEVEN

Information gathering

7.1 Purpose of this stage

The purpose of this stage is to establish the business scope and requirements – the scope for change and the issues that the organisation must address in both its IS strategy and plans for change. The team must gain a full understanding of the current and future business of the organisation and the issues facing it. At this stage, the team begins its strategic thinking, following analysis of interviews and other information gathering. Early thinking about strategic issues, opportunities, collaboration with others, partnerships and so on includes detailed questions about the organisation's mandate and prior options. Throughout, IS is considered as part of business change, not as a separate component.

This is where the identification of issues and assumptions are especially useful tools. It is also useful to identify and carry forward out-of-scope items, which will be referred upwards in due course. In some cases, up to 50% of the resources and timescale of the study could be spent here. It is also useful to look for early, rapid implementation opportunities at this point – often issues are flushed out which have easy, quick tactical solutions; they must not be buried.

7.2 Information gathering

The team gathers material from the following sources:
- documented information
- findings from interviews, focus groups and so on – including perceptions of where the organisation is now
- information about current initiatives and drivers for change
- inputs from other teams and projects such as those working on current initiatives.

Sources of information

The major information sources are likely to be:
- generic strategic issues, such as improving the quality of service
- initial view of the business environment (produced in the *Preparation* stage)
- the organisation's corporate or business strategies and plans
- interviews and focus groups
- working papers produced by the study team
- papers produced for management boards
- other initiatives and studies already underway
- other internal documents, such as Registry files.

If there is no formal corporate or business strategy, time should be allowed during this stage to address those business planning issues necessary for developing the IS strategy. This may draw on short term and informal plans which are implicit in management policies and the activities of the organisation, but which have not been formally defined.

Who to consult

You will need to confirm findings and conclusions with individual managers as a routine part of the interviewing process, and to obtain collective agreement of the interim products.

The circulation of working papers outside the study team is a useful mechanism for exposing the emerging thinking of the team and soliciting feedback from relevant members of the organisation (see Chapter 10, *Topics for working papers*).

Collective agreement could be achieved with focus groups or by holding one or more seminars for senior and top management. These seminars may be linked to a meeting with management to report the results of the *Information gathering* stage (see Section 7.6: *First checkpoint*), and to present the conclusions to take forward to the next stage.

It is important to note that producing and agreeing interim products with management ensures a common understanding of the business and its direction.

Confidentiality

Top and senior management must be able to discuss issues freely with the study team. Respondents should be assured that confidentiality will be respected and that anonymity for respondents will be preserved in study deliverables.

The study may have to consider the implications of confidential organisational business and policy options which cannot be widely discussed. The treatment of such matters has to be arrived at on a case-by-case basis, typically by means of confidential addenda to the main IS strategy study report.

Conducting interviews

In developing the interview list (compiled in the *Preparation* stage) to create an interview programme, you must consider carefully the sequence of interviews in order to make the best use of managers' time. For example, you should try to schedule all the lower level interviews in one part of the business at the same time. Below is a suggested sequence:

1 *Top management* – brief visit to alert them to the purpose of the IS strategy: are there any key issues they wish to raise?
2 *Senior management* – what is their perception of the important issues?
3 *Middle management* – can they amplify the issues and identify any others? (Revisit senior management if inconsistencies emerge)
4 *Top management* – substantive interviews: focus on issues that can only be resolved at this level.

Workshops are an effective means of getting management agreement and consensus on important issues, particularly where business objectives and plans have not yet been formally established.

7.3	Identifying the political and organisational issues

In any organisation, business activity is not governed solely by business considerations; many other factors are involved – for example, personalities, political pressures, organisational structures and employee relations. The IS strategy has to operate in the real world. You will need to identify the issues which affect your organisation. These may be internal to the organisation; they may relate to other organisations or pressure groups with which your organisation interacts; or they may concern government policy. You may also need to consider relationships with business partners and suppliers.

In particular, you should ask the following questions about your organisation:
- what are the drivers for change?
- how are the organisation's responsibilities organised?
- what are the key relationships with other organisations?
- what are the command structures and reporting chains?
- what styles of management are in use?
- who has authority and to what degree?
- what freedoms, constraints, or political imperatives are there?
- are any of the above likely to change in the future?

All of these issues have significant bearing on future options for improved use of IS and on the willingness of the organisation to embrace change. Although the political and organisational issues are not presented to management as an interim product, they are vital in helping you to produce the business drivers and priorities and the models of the business. The issues should also be documented as part of the strategy study report (see Part C, *Products*).

7.4	Business analysis and modelling

The objectives of business analysis are:
- to define the objectives and priorities of the business
- to understand the current and future business and the policies of the organisation.

This analysis extends the scope and depth of the work carried out in the *Preparation* stage. It provides a foundation for all subsequent work. Above all, it works towards a business-oriented strategy.

Identifying objectives and priorities

The main input to this activity is the organisation's corporate objectives and/or business strategy. This strategy may not be formally articulated or may be incomplete, particularly given opportunities opened up by the potential use of IS and its underlying technology. In some cases, a corporate or business strategy may not exist. The study team may provide important input to the development or enhancement of corporate objectives and, consequently, to the development of the business strategy.

The purpose of identifying objectives and priorities is to:
- articulate what the business does and for whom – its customers and stakeholders
- establish its future direction (including changes to the organisation, structure and geography of the major business functions; changing relationships with other organisations; any desired changes in organisational 'culture', and the broad timescales and milestones for changes)
- provide an indication of the timescale for achievement and identify measures of business achievement
- identify the relative importance of the business objectives (and functions) to the success of the business
- identify any objectives arising from outside the organisation, such as central government initiatives, statutory requirements or objectives of partners.

Some of the business objectives of the organisation may have particular timescales or milestones associated with them or may be related to quantified targets, such as financial or other resource limits, desired outcomes, or output targets. Any such objectives should be noted by the study team, since it will be necessary to confirm that the IS strategy demonstrably contributes to the achievement of these objectives.

Analysing the business

Business analysis is not an exact or structured science. The underlying thinking is concerned with gaining an understanding of the way in which the business of the organisation has been, and will be, conducted, and of the imperatives and constraints acting upon it. Many different perspectives may be called for – each providing an understanding of a different facet of the total picture.

The strategy must be resilient to possible future scenarios; if the business or its environment or markets are at all volatile, and forecasting is difficult, a range of scenarios should be identified and evaluated.

The analysis considers the current status of the business, the future direction (as currently perceived by the business management) and other possibilities for future business direction, including those suggested by strategic thinking about the potential impact of IS/IT on the business.

The business analysis activity will be concerned with:
- analysis of the business 'as is', in order to identify how developments in IS/IT can help to improve current operations and business processes
- identification of one or more possible future models of the business, including models based on the exploitation of IS/IT as a vehicle for business change.

The possibilities for future models of the business will be identified from the strategic thinking of the study team and the organisation's management team.

Where a future business model involves the redesign or elimination of current processes, or a change in business direction and the introduction of new processes, the 'as is' analysis will no longer be relevant as a basis for the IS strategy and its supporting information systems architecture and detailed design.

Suggestions for redesign of the business and changes in business direction will need to be presented to the business management and discussed with them in the course of the review and feedback processes in the study. It will be necessary to establish the extent to which the business is willing to initiate and accept radical change, as opposed to step improvements in its current operations. The response of the business to these questions will enable the IS strategy study team to identify both the relevance of the 'as is' analysis to the IS strategy and the need for investigation of future business models in the next stage of the strategy study, or as a post-study activity. For this reason, it is likely that some iteration will have to take place between the business analysis activity and the activity of 'identifying the direction for the future' in the next stage of the study.

Business analysis questions   Analysis and modelling techniques, such as those referred to in the companion volume *Techniques*, can be used to clarify what may be complex real-world situations. The following checklist gives some of the questions you should seek to answer:

- what is the essential role of the business?
- how well does it meet its current objectives?
- what is it trying to do better, cheaper, differently?
- what are the factors that constrain this?
- what is its future direction and how well is it positioned for this change?
- what are the priorities; what makes them priorities; and who sets them?
- how are its activities broken down; how are they currently undertaken and organised?
- what are the main information requirements of the activities and processes?
- how, why and when does the business interrelate with other functions in the organisation?
- how does it interact with outside organisations?
- where and why is there potential for increased efficiency, effectiveness and economy, and how might IS contribute?
- what is the geographic distribution of the organisation's units and business processes?
- what are the requirements for internal communications and data transfer?

The study team should bear in mind that business analysis in the IS strategy study should not be taken to extreme lengths: the object of the exercise is to ensure an adequate understanding of the business processes and their information requirements, not to produce a system specification or design. It should also be remembered that analysis of existing processes may prove to be unnecessary, if the IS strategy identifies scope for process replacement or redesign.

7.5 Current strategies

Review of current strategies for IS, IT and OMP (organisation, management and policies) involves:

- understanding the key messages of the current strategies
- determining the extent to which the documented strategies, have been followed by the organisation
- assessing the successes and failures of the strategies and the extent to which they have contributed to the development of the business
- assessing their fitness for purpose in the current circumstances and the scope for changes in the strategies.

The review of the IT strategy will be limited to assessing its impact on the IS strategy. Detailed review and update of technical aspects of the IT strategy will normally be a separate exercise, as discussed earlier. The study team will need to maintain contact with the IS provider organisations, in order to ensure that the team is maintaining awareness of relevant developments in IT and their potential contribution to the business.

The review of OMP will be limited to those aspects which are relevant to IS management and the business requirements of the organisation, together with the operation of the business/provider relationship. Where some or all of the provider management is in-house, the IS strategy may cover the organisation and management of the in-house unit, and any provider management policies which affect the business.

Reviewing existing IS strategy and IS/IT

Some of the questions you should address in your review are:

- has the previous IS strategy delivered the expected benefits? If not, why not?
- do the priorities for information systems match those of the business? What IS initiatives are underway?
- what are the key information systems?
- what is the extent of existing systems integration?
- are users satisfied with existing systems? What are their requirements in strategic terms?
- what are the costs of the existing systems? Are resources used efficiently?
- how are decisions on IS expenditure made; by whom; and what degree of control and coordination is exercised?
- are the systems and infrastructure capable of meeting new needs?

The study team should produce an inventory of current and planned information systems, including applications under development. The future of these systems will need to be considered in the high level planning phase of the study.

Information to be collected about each of the information systems and applications will include:

- the function of the system and its major sub-systems
- the contribution of the system to the business of the organisation
- the users of the system and their business roles
- the benefits delivered by the system
- its age and status; any developments and enhancements planned, requirements for redevelopment
- related systems and applications; sources and destinations of data; data sharing by the system
- files and databases used
- technology platform, development language, packages used
- the extent to which the system is currently providing adequate support to the business
- the extent to which the system will meet future business requirements
- problems with the system, inefficiencies in operation, gaps in functional coverage
- user satisfaction with the system, ease of use, degree of integration with business processes.

Reviewing policies

Policies relating to IS provide a framework for the way in which information systems will be specified, acquired, implemented, used, managed, supported and enhanced. The purpose of these policies is to provide the backbone of guidance required by users and to ensure consistency in implementing the IS strategy – particularly important where there are several IS providers and/or where other organisations are involved.

Corporate policies

Where individual business units have their own IS strategies, a corporate IS strategy must define the framework in which they will operate. The policies set out in the corporate strategy may require translation and expansion for the component strategies.

The policies address both management and technical issues in providing IS. Benefits management and sourcing are examples of topics for which management policies may be required; IT standards for hardware, software and communications are examples of technical issues. Some policies cover both aspects – for example, security. Annex A, *Management and technical policies*, gives a list of topics for which policies may be needed.

The establishment of policies implies that the organisation will take steps to ensure that they are complied with. Conformance with policies will generally be monitored through procedures defined in the IS strategy. The corporate IS Steering Group or equivalent may wish to participate in the setting, promulgation and monitoring of IS policies.

Policies can be regarded as either 'enabling' or 'restraining'. Enabling policies are those which aim to support, promote and encourage the deployment of effective information systems and services. Restraining policies are those which aim to control or constrain the IS activities in the various parts of the organisation, either for their own good or the greater good of the organisation as a whole.

7.6 Identifying strategic issues

During the *Preparation* and *Information gathering* stages, you will have been forming views on the issues that are potentially strategic for the organisation – that is, the problems or opportunities the organisation must do something about if it is to achieve its business objectives. You now need to make a provisional list of the issues that must be addressed in the IS strategy. These issues will form the basis of the strategic themes in the next stage: *Identifying the direction for the future.* (The companion volume *Techniques* helps you to identify the issues that are important to you.)

7.7 Strategic thinking: identifying the scope for change

Throughout the *Information gathering* stage, the team explores the possibilities for change and the constraints. Questions are raised about the feasibility of working in new ways, requirements to work across organisational boundaries with other public sector organisations and/or strategic partnerships with private sector providers, the opportunities for innovative approaches to exploiting IS and so on. The questions and opportunities will be explored in more depth in the next stage, *Identifying the direction for the future.* But at this point, the study team seeks to identify what is possible – and realistic – for the organisation.

7.8 First checkpoint with management

> **First checkpoint with management**
> The business scope and requirements (baseline for problems, issues and the scope for change) – validation of assumptions

The purpose of this checkpoint is to confirm that the business scope and requirements are complete, accurate and correctly identified. The study team seeks agreement that:

- the business assumptions are correct
- the strategic issues identified by the team reflect the organisation's business drivers and priorities
- the scope for change is within achievable boundaries, although possibilities may include radical change
- business information and support needs and priorities are complete and correct.

The issues that are outside the scope of this study are also identified at this point.

7.9 Practical pointers

Information gathering is all about getting the business view. The process of gathering information depends in part on interviews; observing strict rules of confidentiality will help to find out the real issues. Focus groups open up wider debate of the issues and are a valuable means of ensuring that coverage is complete.

For information gathering, there will be interviews with a number of interested parties. You will need to identify who these are and how many interviews will be required. It may be helpful to categorise interviewees in groups. You should produce a checklist of questions for each category of interviewees. A recommended approach is to use standard interview report and analysis forms to help the study team to check and cross-validate the information collected.

As the study team proceeds through the study, and strategic themes become apparent, interviews become a dialogue with interviewees, a way of taking them along with you and getting feedback and buy-in. So it is much more than just information gathering.

Focus groups, such as cross-organisation workshops, give staff the opportunity to meet and share common issues and problems; it involves them and helps to achieve buy-in. It is also a way of establishing consensus and generating creative ideas. One approach is to ask each business manager to nominate someone who is not at management level as a member of a focus group. They may be able to contribute creative ideas on what needs to change. They may tell you things that management cannot/will not tell you about what the organisation really is and how it might change.

Information gathering: lessons learned from recent studies
- value of checklists to ensure consistency/quality
- value of working papers to stimulate thought and discussion
- wider circulation of working papers to expose emerging thinking and conclusions
- value of interviews to impart information and generate commitment
- value of workshops and focus groups to involve staff, provide feedback and ensure buy-in
- strategic thinking: need for creativity, divergent thinking
- 'traceability' – documentation that explains *why* things are being done and the options to move forward.

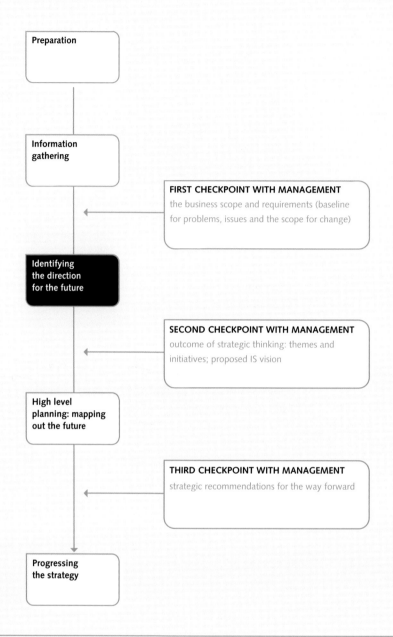

Preparation

Information
gathering

FIRST CHECKPOINT WITH MANAGEMENT
the business scope and requirements (baseline
for problems, issues and the scope for change)

Identifying
the direction
for the future

SECOND CHECKPOINT WITH MANAGEMENT
outcome of strategic thinking: themes and
initiatives; proposed IS vision

High level
planning: mapping
out the future

THIRD CHECKPOINT WITH MANAGEMENT
strategic recommendations for the way forward

Progressing
the strategy

Activities
- identify strategic themes – what will
  shape the future direction?
- identify candidates for action –
  radical thinking, brainstorming the
  options

In parallel:
- define IS architectures – process, data
- develop and confirm IS vision

Products
Definition of themes
Candidate projects for each theme
Options for implementation
Broad architecture and standards
Vision statement

CHAPTER EIGHT

Identifying the direction for the future

8.1 Purpose of this stage

The purpose of this stage is to identify the direction for the organisation's future deployment of IS as part of business change, while carrying forward the IS/IT that is already committed. This is a critical, complex stage that needs to take account of the implications for the future. Business management and the study team take a radical approach to the question "How can we do things differently?". The team members consider the need for the organisation to work together and share information (and processes) with organisations in and outside the public sector. They focus on business change: will IS be an enabler or a blocker to progress? They address the need to cope with uncertainty – both in the business environment and in technological change. Activities may need to be done in parallel, and iterated to ensure rigour and to generate new ideas. The goal is to define the strategic direction in terms of themes and to identify realistic options for progressing the themes.

Summary

In this stage, the work of the study team continues the strategic thinking started in the previous stage and then moves to strategic planning, with the development of high level plans for realisation of the strategy.

The process of strategic thinking in this stage involves the divergent activity of opening up possibilities and exploring new ways of doing things. It covers:
- identification of strategic themes, including responses to the strategic issues identified in the previous stage
- identification of candidates for action to progress each of the strategic themes.

The study team moves into a process of strategic planning, involving analysis, selection and convergent thinking. It covers:
- making selections from the candidates for action, to constitute one or more possible portfolios for action
- detailed planning of the preferred portfolio for action, as part of the wider business planning of the organisation.

8.2 Identifying strategic themes

Strategic themes are identified – what will shape the future direction?

Identification of strategic themes follows on from the identification of strategic issues. Issues are the strategic problems, or opportunities, confronting the organisation; the themes between them represent the organisation's response to the issues, where the response includes a major IS/IT component. Issues for which IS/IT does not contribute to the solution will not be addressed in the IS strategy, but will be resolved through other aspects of the organisation's business strategy.

A theme in the IS strategy will be a significant topic, related to strategic change in IS, IT or OMP, which is of concern to the business management of the organisation. It is a topic which the business management will wish to keep under review for the foreseeable future, as part of the task of monitoring the performance of the business and the achievement of its business objectives. For the IS strategy, themes may be expressed in terms of significant changes or developments required in, for example:

- strategic information systems
- exploitation of high-potential technology
- IS/IT architecture or infrastructure
- scope or delivery of desktop services
- external communications and interworking
- managing the information resource of the organisation
- IS/IT management or organisation issues
- IS development and the development lifecycle
- sourcing and procurement issues
- major operational information systems
- IS/IT support for redesigned business processes
- services offered to customers or the public.

It should be possible to express the essence of the IS strategy in no more than four to six broad themes. A description of a theme will include:

- the reason why the theme is strategically important to the organisation
- the strategic issues which this theme helps to address
- the main changes or developments which the organisation will expect to achieve within the theme, and the direction in which this theme will take the organisation.

The themes identified for the IS strategy will, between them, encompass the strategic changes required in IS, IT or OMP to support the programme of business change agreed by the organisation's business management. Some iteration may be required between the discussions on business change and the identification of strategic themes.

The study team should confirm with business management that the identified themes are appropriate to take forward in the strategy study as the basis for subsequent stages.

Developments in organisation, management and policies

Strategic changes in OMP may include changes in:

- the roles and responsibilities for management of IS in the organisation
- developments in the *Intelligent Customer* function or equivalent (see the CCTA guide *The Informed Partner*)

- the composition and Terms of Reference of cross-departmental committees concerned with IS strategy and planning, such as the IS Steering Committee
- arrangements for budgeting and charging for IS/IT supplies and services.

8.3 Identifying candidate projects to realise each theme

A theme identifies a broad area of concern within which the organisation will need to plan a variety of activities in order to achieve the changes or improvements required to move the organisation, or some aspect of its IS/IT, in the desired direction. For each strategic theme, it is necessary to identify ways in which these changes might be realised. This involves the search for candidate projects to realise the themes. As a first step in breaking down each broad theme into candidates for action, the study team should address the following questions for each theme:

- what are the practical alternatives, 'dreams' or 'visions' we might pursue to address this strategic theme, achieve this goal, or realise this scenario?
- what are the barriers to the realisation of these alternatives, dreams or visions?
- what major proposals might we pursue to achieve these alternatives, dreams or visions directly, or to overcome the barriers to their realisation?
- what major actions with existing staff and resources (as the starting point) must be taken within the next year or so to make essential progress on this theme?

It may be useful to identify some broad 'areas of activity' as a stepping stone to lower-level 'candidates for action'.

The answers to these questions will lead the study team to the identification of a number of candidate projects which could contribute to each theme. This involves creative, divergent thinking and may take the team outside the realm of IS/IT: many themes will involve wider programmes of business change, of which IS/IT will be only one component.

For example, in a recent IS strategy exercise one of the strategic themes was identified as: "How can we maximise the benefits obtained from our existing and future investment in IS/IT?". Areas of activity identified as contributing to the achievement of this theme were:

- implementing a benefits management programme
- integrating process improvement and IS implementation exercises
- developing and maintaining user skills
- sharing developments among units of the organisation
- proactive scanning of opportunities for innovative technologies.

In the example, each of these areas was broken down further into a number of specific candidates for action, each of which could constitute a bounded project or activity.

Identification of candidates for action is a continuation of strategic thinking, since it is concerned with finding options and possibilities for progressing the themes.

However, it can also be regarded as a preliminary step leading to the high level planning arising from the strategy process.

A candidate for action could be any activity or development – including supply of technology – which would require resources of any kind from the organisation or its IS supplier/s. Typically, a candidate for action will appear as a proposal for a defined package of work which (if approved) will be established as a project; or an allocation of resources assigned to meet a specific objective or produce a defined output. A candidate for action should be specified in such a way that it can, in principle, be scoped, costed and scheduled as a discrete resource or activity. At this stage, the candidates for action constitute a 'shopping list' of developments, which will be subject to analysis, prioritisation and selection in the next stage.

A candidate for action could be, for example:
- implementing a new IS development
- introduction of new or updated technology
- initiation of a study or consultancy
- changes in organisational structure or function
- changes in management or other responsibilities
- changes in administration
- allocation of resources to an ongoing task or responsibility
- changing a relationship with an external organisation
- undertaking a procurement of supplies or services
- introducing new policies or procedures
- setting up a Task Force
- setting up a training programme
- preparing and disseminating information.

Where a candidate for action has been identified as a study (such as a feasibility study) it may be possible to scope the study itself, but the outcome of the study will, in principle, be unknown at this stage. To this extent, detailed planning beyond the study will not be possible, or will be subject to major uncertainty. Similar considerations will apply to candidates for action such as scoping studies, benchmarking exercises, pilot implementations and technology trials. Once the outcome of these activities is known (which will be after completion of the IS strategy study), the detailed implementation plans at that time will be updated to incorporate the decisions based on the outcome of the study or trial.

The candidates for action are derived from consideration of the strategic themes. They are oriented to strategic objectives and will not necessarily address IS/IT-based activities which do not have a strategic dimension. The sum total of IS/IT-based activities required by the business will include a range of other calls on IS/IT resources.

The candidates for action will need to be considered together with other calls on resources, such as developments which are regarded as necessary but not strategic. These will include developments required to satisfy new statutory requirements, non-discretionary developments, development of applications which do not make a significant organisation-wide contribution to business objectives, ongoing support and maintenance of existing facilities, and upgrades needed to replace obsolete technology. These developments will be planned and prioritised, together with developments arising from the initiatives.

8.4 Defining IS architecture

The process of defining and refining the IS architecture is carried out in parallel with the definition of themes, and candidates for action. The strategic IS architecture maps out the key information systems to be developed or maintained, the main data holdings in the organisation and the relationships between them. The strategic IS architecture will be designed to support the initiatives under the IS strategy, and the candidate projects will include the activities necessary to implement the changes required in the IS architecture under the strategy. Realisation of a new IS architecture could itself be one of the themes of the strategy. This task covers the following activities:

- assessing the relevance of existing IS architecture to candidates for action
- defining target IS architecture
- assessing the implication for IS strategy (will the existing architecture require major change, perhaps becoming the subject of a new theme?)
- assessing the implications for the supporting IT architecture (what will need to change?)
- defining the required changes.

The IS architecture arising from the strategy review will not be finalised until the high level planning has been completed in the next stage of the study.

8.5 Defining the IS vision

The IS vision summarises the desired future for information systems in the organisation; it expresses 'where we want to be' in relation to the contribution of IS to the business success of the organisation. It indicates the areas of significant change which will be effected in IS, and the desired outcome of such changes and developments.

It can be difficult to produce a meaningful and useful IS vision statement. The statement should avoid the extremes of:

- a bland high level 'vision' of pervasive IS support, which could apply to almost any organisation
- a detailed catalogue of specific planned developments, which increasingly becomes invalidated as circumstances and implementation plans change.

Two approaches to the development of an IS vision statement can be suggested:

- where the business strategy of the organisation is clearly based on specific targets and milestones, with corresponding IS objectives, the contribution of the IS strategy can be expressed in terms of the achievement of those objectives. The IS vision will then be of a situation in which the IS high level objectives have been met. For example:
  - by 200x we will be conducting x% of our transactions with the public through electronic media
  - by 200y all of our staff will have desktop access to in-house information services
  - by 200z we will have established joint facilities for input of forms and sharing of client data with organisations P and Q.
- since the strategic themes, if correctly identified, will address the strategic issues facing the organisation, the realisation of the themes will lead the organisation in the right direction for its IS/IT. The IS vision can then be expressed in terms of the outcome of pursuing the themes of the IS strategy. The vision statement can be constructed by considering what the situation will be as a result of progressing each of the themes in the IS strategy. In this case, the IS vision statement will be produced after the themes have been defined and agreed with business management.

8.6 Second checkpoint with management

> **Second checkpoint with management**
> Outcome of strategic thinking: themes; the IS vision

These approaches are not mutually exclusive and can be combined, if appropriate, to construct a meaningful IS vision statement.

This checkpoint concludes the *Identifying future the direction* stage. Management is asked to confirm the outcome of the strategic thinking so far, validating the themes and the proposed IS vision.

The business case for the strategy is agreed at this checkpoint, based on the themes. This business case is qualitative and business oriented. The business case for the high level plans is presented later, at the third checkpoint. It is essential to separate the business case for the strategy from the business case for particular planned developments.

Business case for the IS strategy

The business case for the IS strategy will be a justification for the strategy in business terms, taking into account, in broad terms, the financial implications as well as relevant qualitative issues. For example, it will seek to demonstrate that:

- the themes for the IS strategy have been correctly identified (that is, they are indeed 'strategic' for the organisation, and there are no others which are more important)

- the IS strategy adequately addresses the issues confronting the organisation (insofar as these issues are amenable to IS/IT-based solutions)
- the IS strategy supports and promotes the wider business strategy of the organisation
- the business assumptions on which the IS strategy is based are reasonable
- the IS strategy adopts an acceptable position in relation to the risk and uncertainty with which it must deal
- the benefits which will be derived from the realisation of the IS strategy are in line with wider business objectives
- the IS strategy is realisable and politically acceptable (for example, to the stakeholders in the organisation)
- the mechanisms and procedures for monitoring and progressing the IS strategy within the organisation will be effective.

Annex B, *Business case development*, summarises the development of individual business cases, focusing on the need to demonstrate business and strategic 'fit' with the overall direction of the business and IS strategies.

It is unlikely that the business case for the IS strategy will be supported by detailed financial analysis. It may not be meaningful to assess the 'value for money of the IS strategy', since there will not always be detailed information about money in the IS strategy. The business case for the IS strategy provides a defined context for the individual developments through which the strategy will be progressed.

8.7 Practical pointers

At this stage, in particular, there must be creative, radical thinking and a willingness to explore new ways of doing things. The switch from analysis to creative synthesis to innovative thinking is very different from earlier approaches, which concentrated on the opportunities for improvement rather than a completely new look at what is possible. The study team must be able to do this. Experience has shown that benchmarking studies with similar organisations, not just in the public sector, often suggest new approaches that are worth considering.

> Identifying the future direction: strategic thinking
> - how we work is as important as what business we are in. In a time when technology is challenging our performance and the way we work, strategic advantage is likely to come from transforming the organisation, its processes and practices
> - techniques for creative, divergent thinking are described in the companion volume *Techniques*
> - CCTA's guidance on benchmarking and business process reengineering may suggest new possibilities.

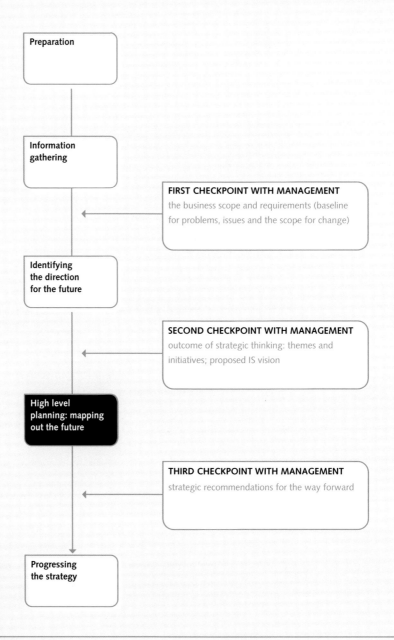

Preparation

Information gathering

FIRST CHECKPOINT WITH MANAGEMENT
the business scope and requirements (baseline for problems, issues and the scope for change)

Identifying the direction for the future

SECOND CHECKPOINT WITH MANAGEMENT
outcome of strategic thinking: themes and initiatives; proposed IS vision

High level planning: mapping out the future

THIRD CHECKPOINT WITH MANAGEMENT
strategic recommendations for the way forward

Progressing the strategy

Activities
- Strategy realisation: high level plans
- Strategy definition
- Identify and formulate policies
- Planning for organisation, management and policies

Products
High level plans for action: strategic, ongoing, other
Recommended way forward
Strategy statement
Plans and policies for organisation and management; sourcing; architecture and IT standards etc

CHAPTER NINE

High level planning

9.1 Purpose of this stage

The purpose of this stage is to map out the future development and deployment of IS/IT in the organisation, in the form of high level plans (portfolios of IS/IT-related activities and developments) emerging from the strategic thinking. Business management leads the planning activity, with support from the study team. High level planning includes consideration of revised arrangements for organisation, management and policies for IS/IT. The process follows on from the identification of candidates for action, and involves the prioritisation and selection of some of the candidates for action – and the rejection of others – for inclusion in the current high level plans for implementation. The high level plans will also include committed activities, non-strategic developments and non-discretionary developments, as described earlier.

Summary

High level planning marks the transition from strategic thinking to strategic planning. The divergent thinking of earlier stages now gives way to convergent thinking, which translates the options and possibilities identified in earlier stages into defined profiles for development and realistic, achievable plans. However, the study team must be prepared to return, as necessary, to earlier stages if new possibilities present themselves at this late stage. The process of high level planning may uncover additional options or constraints which have to be taken into account, and may force a revision of earlier conclusions.

Planning for organisation, management and policies

The high level planning activity will consider the need for new or changed arrangements for organisation, management and policies (OMP) for IS/IT, which were investigated in the previous stage. Any developments, organisational changes, or changes in roles and responsibilities will be considered together with other candidates for action, to form part of the preferred portfolio of developments produced in this stage. The details of changes and developments in this area will depend partly on the scope and nature of the IS/IT developments which constitute the high level plan.

9.2 Perspectives on planning

The high level plans for IS/IT developments arising from the IS strategy must be considered from two perspectives: the business and IS/IT delivery (providers). Both of these perspectives must be taken into account, and both sides must be satisfied with the outcome of the high level planning.

From the point of view of business management, IS/IT developments will generally be seen not as an end in themselves, but as contributing to wider programmes of business change and to the achievement of business objectives. Planning for business-related IS/IT developments must then be seen as an integral component of the wider planning activity within the business – this may take place centrally, or within each business unit, or in some combination. The scope, timing, resourcing and implementation of business-related IS/IT developments will depend on the requirements of the relevant part of the business. Plans for IS/IT-related developments must be designed to fit in with the business plan of which it is a component, and must reflect the priorities of the business. From this perspective, the IS strategy does not deliver an all-encompassing plan for organisational IS/IT; the business view is of a number of activities and developments, each of which contributes to one or more business functions, and for which the responsibility lies with the business.

Some developments – such as the universal roll-out of desktop facilities – will affect the business as a whole and will need to be planned centrally. The business will also wish to take a coordinated view of requirements which affect all business units, such as the sharing of information, implementation of management policies, approaches to electronic records management, and facilitating internal communications. Other developments – such as those concerned with the implementation of technical infrastructure – will not be directly visible to the business and will be the responsibility of the provider organisation/s. But where an IS/IT development is directly related to a business unit, the business and planning responsibilities should go hand-in-hand.

Provider considerations

From the point of view of IS/IT delivery, the provider organisation (whether in-house or external, or a combination) will need to consider the technical and resourcing implications of all possible demands for IS/IT. The sum total of provider activities and developments in the high level plans will need to be considered in the light of factors such as:

- demands on provider staff resources and available skills for IS/IT delivery
- requirements for infrastructure developments and enhancements
- existing commitments on resources
- funds available for purchase of supplies and services
- dependencies and relationships between developments
- timetables for procurement
- implications for support and maintenance.

The provider/s will need to consider the implications of all the high level plans, including developments which are the responsibility of the business and developments which are a provider responsibility. The review of sourcing policies in the study will have considered how the provider is to be organised, and the division of provider responsibilities between in-house and external providers.

9.3 Components of high level plans

The high level plans for IS/IT developments arising from the IS strategy study comprise:

- high level plans for IS/IT developments in specific business areas of the organisation. These plans will be components of wider plans for business development and change in individual business units; and will be the responsibility of individual business managers
- high level plans for corporate IS/IT developments and policies affecting the organisation as a whole, such as changes in infrastructure facilities, policies for information management and organisation-wide applications. These plans will be the responsibility of a designated manager on behalf of the whole organisation
- high level plans for developments in the delivery of provider facilities, such as the technical infrastructure or the organisation of in-house service delivery. These plans will be the responsibility of the provider management.

The development of high level plans will involve consultation between the business and the provider/s. Some iteration and accommodation will be needed between the requirements of the business and the resources and capabilities of the provider. Individual business units will need to become involved in the discussions where the high level plans for IS/IT are components of their wider business plans.

In many organisations, an advisory unit (in central government, often titled the *Intelligent Customer Function*) has been established to manage the relationships between the business and its in-house and external providers of IS/IT.

9.4 Factors in high level planning

Decisions on the selection of the portfolio of developments and activities to be included in high level plans will need to take into account the views of both the business and provider organisations, as described in the previous section. In addition, the high level planning process will need to take into consideration factors such as:

- the ability and willingness of the organisation to cope with business and technical change
- requirements for non-discretionary developments which must be included in the plans
- developments and pressures in the environment which may affect the priorities for implementation
- the scale of the benefits to be derived from individual developments
- the timescales for achievement of benefits and the desire of the organisation to demonstrate 'quick hits' in IS/IT implementation
- the risks associated with particular developments (business and technical risks), and the total amount of risk which the organisation wishes to assume
- timetables and resources required for procurement exercises.

These factors will all contribute to the process of selection and prioritisation through which the high level plan is developed and agreed with the business.

9.5 The high level planning process

The high level planning process starts with lists of:

- the candidates for action identified for realisation of of the themes
- other existing or possible calls on IS/IT provider resources (or business resources if appropriate) arising from existing and committed developments, non-discretionary activities and non-strategic developments.

As a first step, it should be possible to eliminate some of the candidates for action at this stage as being inappropriate or infeasible (but they should be left for future reference, since they may become realistic candidates at some future point). Similarly, it may be possible to decide to eliminate some existing commitments or developments as unnecessary under the new IS strategy. Each of the remaining activities or developments should then be scoped in terms of:

- estimated resources and costs for completion (these will be subject to wide margins of error at this stage)
- expected outcome and benefits arising
- implications for IT infrastructure and support
- dependencies on other developments or on other components of business plans
- constraints on timing – for example, this must be finished by a specified milestone date in the business plan.

Non-strategic IS/IT projects should, as part of their plans, include statements about the way in which they are expected, eventually, to fit into the organisation's IS strategy. For example, there may be interim solutions until a more strategic solution is practicable. It is essential that any non-strategic IS developments are authorised by the relevant IS strategy 'theme manager'.

At this stage in high level planning, it must be recognised that any estimates produced in the scoping exercise will be very approximate, and in some cases it will not be possible to produce credible estimates at all. In addition, where a large number of activities has to be considered, the effort available for producing the scoping information will be limited. It must be borne in mind that estimates produced at this stage will be used primarily to assist the study team and business management in the selection of a preferred implementation profile, and not as the basis for assigning resources. Firmer estimates for each of the selected activities will be generated when they are subjected to low level planning at a later stage.

High level planning includes consideration of revised arrangements for organisation, management and policies for IS/IT.

Where a study activity is identified, it will not be possible to arrive at realistic estimates for the resultant activity until the study team has reported.

9.6 Implementation profiles

The high level planning task is, then, to construct one or more profiles for implementation, combining selected activities and developments in programmes of work which:

- meet requirements and targets and satisfy constraints, as specified by the business
- present acceptable cost and benefit profiles
- are consistent with overall business strategy and plans for change
- can be resourced and delivered by supplier organisations
- are technically achievable with acceptable risk.

Two approaches are possible for the construction of development profiles:

- define one recommended, or preferred, profile and present that to management for endorsement
- develop a small number of implementation profiles, setting out the implications of each one, and present them to management for consideration and selection.

In the latter case, the profiles would be constructed to deliver outcomes which differ in terms of business focus, phasing of developments, profile of costs and benefits, impact on infrastructure, degree of risk, and so on. Management should provide guidance to the study team on which of these approaches it should adopt.

Link to Programme Management

The preferred profile will be taken forward by both the organisation and its provider/s. The organisation will integrate the various components of the IS/IT plans into its projects and programmes for business change and development, using a formal approach such as CCTA's Programme Management. The IS/IT provider/s will use the plans to project the requirements for IS/IT development, service delivery, support, procurement and changes in provider organisation, management and policies.

Strategy definition

The IS strategy is formally defined in the *strategy statement*. This is the most important deliverable from the IS strategy study. It is a declaratory statement of the strategic direction for top and senior management agreement. It should be communicated to all staff, as it stresses the value of the strategy, in business terms, to the organisation as a whole.

An example structure for the strategy statement is provided in Annex D, *Example of structure of an IS strategy statement*.

9.7 Third checkpoint with management

Third checkpoint with management

Strategic recommendations for the way forward.

The third checkpoint is to agree the results of the strategic planning, to select or approve the preferred profile for business change and/or agree the overall high level plans, which will form the basis of programmes of change.

The business case for the high level plans is presented at this checkpoint. It is based on the scoping information presented with the plans as described above. Costs and benefits for proposed developments are estimated *approximately* where possible; these form the basis for the high level plans. But it should be emphasised that there is not a single high level plan; there are plans for IS/IT developments in each of the business units, and each area of the business will need to produce its own justification for the developments for which it is responsible. So, there will be multiple business cases (see Annex B, *Business case development*, for more information on the business case) presented at this checkpoint, for:

- individual business areas
- corporate developments
- provider developments.

9.8 Detailed planning

Detailed planning of individual developments is outside the scope of the strategy study. It will be undertaken for each development by the business unit or provider organisation responsible for the development. Where a business unit has responsibility for the development, input will be required from providers to provide the necessary technical expertise for the development of detailed plans, which will need to be integrated with wider business planning. Business cases for individual developments will be the responsibility of the units doing the planning and who are accountable for the expenditure.

9.9 Practical pointers

Planning at this stage is at a high level only and is weighted to non-financial benefit and risks, success criteria and performance measures. It is not a tactical plan describing costs, resources and overall spend on IS/IT. It requires convergent thinking – that is, bringing together all the strands of possible candidates for action, evaluating and selecting options and brigading them into programmes of business change, together with all the current/ongoing IS/IT to which the organisation is already committed.

> Outcome of the study: where next?
> - ensure that the organisation distinguishes:
>   - strategy statement
>   - strategy study report (see section 11.2)
>   - plans for implementation of *business* change, not just IS/IT
> - ensure continuing ownership of the strategy by management
> - establish organisational responsibilities for progressing the strategic themes
> - identify follow-up activities such as further studies, detailed planning.

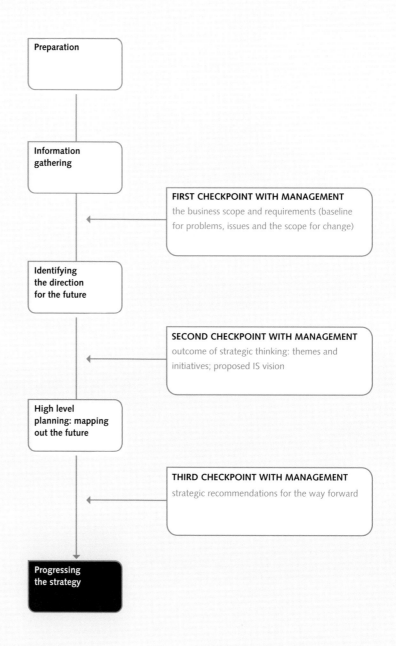

Preparation

Information gathering

FIRST CHECKPOINT WITH MANAGEMENT
the business scope and requirements (baseline for problems, issues and the scope for change)

Identifying the direction for the future

SECOND CHECKPOINT WITH MANAGEMENT
outcome of strategic thinking: themes and initiatives; proposed IS vision

High level planning: mapping out the future

THIRD CHECKPOINT WITH MANAGEMENT
strategic recommendations for the way forward

Progressing the strategy

Ongoing strategic management
Taking strategic decisions
Updating the strategy and themes
Updating plans as required

CHAPTER TEN

Progressing the IS strategy

After the IS strategy has been formulated and adopted by the organisation, it must be kept continually up to date. The strategy process is continuous, both for the IS strategy and for the business strategy of which it is a component. The conduct of an IS strategy study or review, and the delivery of an IS strategy statement, are milestones in the strategy process, not end-points. Strategic decisions will need to be taken as new public sector policies and initiatives arise, as the organisation itself changes and develops, as new technologies become available and as IS/IT developments under the strategy have an increasing impact on the business of the organisation. As the Chinese general Sun Tzu observed, "no strategy survives contact with the enemy". To continue to be effective, an IS strategy must be updated to accommodate changing circumstances. (Progression of the strategy is explored in detail in the companion guide *Strategic Management of Information Systems*.)

10.1 Strategy and plans

This chapter explains the key principles for ensuring that the IS strategy continues to be responsive to the business needs of the organisation. In the context of this chapter, the IS strategy should be taken to mean the strategic themes and their associated programmes and projects, rather than a strategy document. Thus, the IS strategy, as a collective framework for programmes and projects, has high level targets, milestones and risks that need to be monitored closely.

The distinction between making strategy and planning was discussed in Chapter 2, *Overview: the IS strategy and its formulation*. Following the high level planning phase of the strategy study, detailed plans will be drawn up for the implementation of the selected 'candidates for action'. These plans will be implemented in a number of projects or programmes of activity, either as IS/IT activities or by being integrated into wider activities of business change.

Monitoring the progress of individual projects or programmes will be a function of the project management or Programme Management procedures established for these activities. Reports on progress will be fed upwards in the organisation to the business managers responsible for the business programmes, or to the IS/IT providers of infrastructure developments. Where a development is contributing to the progress of a theme of the IS strategy, the relevant 'theme manager' will also need to be kept informed of progress. Within a project or programme, changes to the plan may be made at any time, as a result of changes in requirements, rescheduling to accommodate problems with resourcing, or changes in scope. Such changes will be handled through the normal change control procedures in the project or programme.

10.2 Who is involved?   Monitoring the progress of the IS strategy is the responsibility of senior business management, as part of their overall responsibility for the realisation of the business strategy of the organisation. This chapter discusses how the progress of the IS strategy should be monitored, and how the results of the monitoring are fed back into the strategy process and the detailed planning and implementation procedures.

10.3 Monitoring the IS strategy   Review of the IS strategy is part of the processes and procedures for reviewing the performance of the business as a whole against its strategy and objectives. Reviews of the IS strategy should, therefore, be seen in the context of performance management for the various aspects of the business, as described in the companion guidance *Performance management*. Every review of the IS strategy will lead to action being taken to ensure that the strategy is on course and under control.

The questions which the management of the organisation should be asking about the progress of the IS strategy are similar to those they would regularly ask about the development of the business in relation to the overall business strategy. Typical questions for monitoring the IS strategy are:

- do the themes and policies of the IS strategy continue to reflect the business strategy and the business issues facing the organisation? Are any changes needed in the list of themes or policies? What changes within and outside the organisation do we need to take into account?
- what progress has been achieved within each of the themes of the IS strategy? Are any changes required in the scope of any of the themes? Are the areas of activity for the themes and the portfolios of IS/IT developments still appropriate?
- what performance targets and milestones are defined for the IS strategy, and have they been met? Are they still relevant?
- what benefits for the business are being achieved through the IS strategy? Are the desired outcomes of the IS strategy being delivered as expected?
- do any of the current IS/IT-related projects or programmes need senior management attention?
- do any risks in the current IS strategy need to be brought to the attention of senior management? Have there been any changes in the risks identified in the IS strategy or any of the themes?
- are any changes required in the arrangements for management of IS/IT in the organisation, or in relationships with external suppliers and service providers?
- is there any need to change priorities, business emphasis, allocation of resources or responsibilities for IS/IT-related activities?

Performance measures   As a result of the continuous review of progress for the IS strategy, actions to be taken could include:

- changes to the themes of the IS strategy, as discussed below
- changes in the allocation of resources to current IS/IT activities

- changes to the current portfolios of IS/IT development
- changes to policies for IS/IT, or the development of new policies
- changes in organisation or management for IS/IT, including external provision
- changes on the 'customer' side, such as changes in business plans or processes.

Where relevant, the requirements for the necessary changes will be passed down to the individual projects and programmes, or business units, for implementation.

10.4 Themes in the IS strategy

The IS strategy is focused around the strategic themes and the areas of activity within each theme through which the theme is being progressed. Major changes in the IS strategy reflect changes in the themes. A major change would be the addition or deletion of a theme, while a less radical change could be the addition or removal of an area of activity, or individual activity, from the scope of a theme.

The addition of a theme to the IS strategy would signify that the business management regards this IS/IT-related topic as of major strategic importance to the organisation, as described earlier in this guide. Associated with the new theme would be defined areas of activity related to IS, IT or OMP, and specific work packages selected from the 'candidates for action' identified in the review.

Removal of a theme from the IS strategy does not signify that this topic is no longer of any concern to the organisation; it signifies that the topic is no longer strategic. For example, a theme may be based around the introduction of a new technology with significant implications for the conduct of the organisation's business. As this theme is progressed, the technology is introduced as part of a major process of business change, closely monitored by the business management. As the technology 'beds in' and becomes accepted by the organisation and its customers, and the associated business changes are implemented and absorbed by the organisation, this topic becomes 'business as usual' and the strategic importance of the technology diminishes. At this point, the theme can be removed from the IS strategy, and the issue for management may become one of deciding how to maintain and eventually replace an obsolescent technology. A similar progression of a theme could relate to the response of the organisation to a current government-wide initiative, or to any other issue facing the organisation.

10.5 Who is involved?

Review of the progress in the IS strategy takes place regularly by the senior management forum charged with the management of the strategy. This could be a Steering Group established to manage the IS strategy, or it could be the senior management group, or Management Board, taking the IS strategy as a regular topic on its normal business agenda. In either case, the representation on this group should be predominantly from the business side of the organisation, and the chair of the group should be a senior business representative.

It is essential to ensure that each theme in the IS strategy is progressed. The suggested approach is to identify an individual who is responsible for coordinating and reporting progress on each theme to senior management. It may be appropriate to appoint a 'champion', or 'theme manager', for each theme, tasked with ensuring the planning and coordination of activities across the organisation and across projects, to progress the theme.

For formal annual reviews of the IS strategy, senior management will have a role in the oversight of the project and approval of the deliverables, as discussed in Chapter 5, *The strategy study: getting started.*

10.6 When is the IS strategy reviewed?

The Steering Group reviews progress on the IS strategy at every meeting – typically every two months. It is unlikely that there will be frequent requirements to make radical changes to the IS strategy – indeed, it would be unsettling for the business and the IS/IT providers if the themes of the strategy were subject to continuous change. However, when the business identifies new issues which it has to deal with, it will be necessary to consider the possible contribution of a strategic IS/IT-related response, as described in Chapter 3, *Strategic issues and strategic themes.* The response could be a change in the themes of the IS strategy, new or updated policies, or changes in organisation and management for IS/IT.

The need to consider major reviews of the IS strategy could arise from a number of sources.

Changes in the business environment

Major developments in the business environment of the organisation could prompt a radical review of the IS strategy. The developments could be, for example, new government initiatives, changes in legislation, changes in customer requirements, or changes in the rules governing allocation of resources to the organisation.

Changes within the organisation

The organisation may be undertaking a programme of major reorganisation or restructuring, or the addition or loss of significant business functions. There is likely to be a requirement for radical rethinking of IS/IT provision and the role of IS/IT in business support. These requirements could suggest new themes for the IS strategy.

Developments in technology

As discussed earlier, the IS strategy emerges from a combination of business requirements which prompt an IS/IT-based response and IS/IT initiatives which can suggest responses from the business. The availability of new technologies promising business benefits for the organisation can give rise to new themes for the IS strategy. Developments based on new technologies may start as experimental activities; if successful, these activities could give rise to major programmes of business change.

Outcomes of strategic developments

It is impossible to predict in detail the outcome of developments undertaken within the IS strategy. Many projects and programmes of change will have consequences which were not planned or predicted when the activity was initiated. The organisation must be alert to the identification of unplanned benefits, and to the potential of IS/IT emerging from current projects and operational systems. New themes for the IS strategy may be suggested by building on the unanticipated consequences of current developments.

In addition to the regular monitoring of the IS strategy by the Steering Group, it is advisable to undertake a formal review of the IS strategy on an annual basis. This major review would follow the framework and activities suggested in this guidance, tailored to circumstances of the review. It would result in an updated statement of IS strategy for the organisation. If the IS strategy has been kept under continuous review by the Steering Group, as suggested earlier, much of the activity described in this guidance will be unnecessary, since the strategic themes will have been kept in step with business requirements. If the annual review of the IS strategy coincides with or follows a major review of business strategy, then a more comprehensive approach to the IS strategy review will be required.

10.7 Monitoring performance

At the level of the IS strategy, there may be strategic targets identified for the achievement of milestones for development, perhaps linked to organisation-wide or government-wide targets. For example, the government's targets for electronic transactions are likely to be reflected in the organisation's IS strategy, and progress towards these targets will be monitored by business management. There may also be targets for the coverage of desktop IT facilities throughout the organisation, or for the availability of internal services on-line within the organisation.

Detailed performance targets and measures for outputs from the IS strategy would not normally be appropriate. The IS strategy is a high level statement of objectives for aspects of the business, and progress in its achievement will be measured in terms of intermediate and long-term business outcomes rather than short-term outputs and deliverables. The latter are the concern of the individual projects and programmes forming the portfolio of developments arising from the IS strategy. Reports on outcomes from the IS strategy will be characterised by the questions listed in section 10.2 *Monitoring the IS strategy.*

The role of performance targets and performance measures in performance management for the business is discussed in the companion guidance *Performance Management.*

PART C
Products

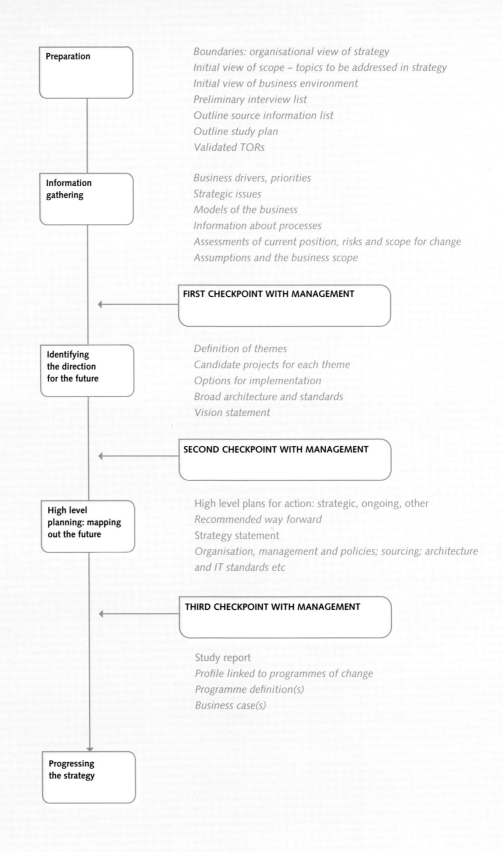

Preparation

Boundaries: organisational view of strategy
Initial view of scope – topics to be addressed in strategy
Initial view of business environment
Preliminary interview list
Outline source information list
Outline study plan
Validated TORs

Information gathering

Business drivers, priorities
Strategic issues
Models of the business
Information about processes
Assessments of current position, risks and scope for change
Assumptions and the business scope

FIRST CHECKPOINT WITH MANAGEMENT

Identifying the direction for the future

Definition of themes
Candidate projects for each theme
Options for implementation
Broad architecture and standards
Vision statement

SECOND CHECKPOINT WITH MANAGEMENT

High level planning: mapping out the future

High level plans for action: strategic, ongoing, other
Recommended way forward
Strategy statement
Organisation, management and policies; sourcing; architecture and IT standards etc

THIRD CHECKPOINT WITH MANAGEMENT

Study report
Profile linked to programmes of change
Programme definition(s)
Business case(s)

Progressing the strategy

CHAPTER ELEVEN

Products overview

This chapter provides an overview of the products that will be developed during the strategy study. Some are permanent documents; others are lower level working papers.

Depending on the scale of the study, many products may be a few brief paragraphs or a complex document comprising several pages of detailed text.

11.1 Different types of product

The different types of product can be categorised as follows:

- *formal deliverables from the study* – strategy statement, study report, high level plans
- *annexes to deliverables* – for example, annexes to the strategy statement
- *supporting documents that are maintained and updated as required* – such as policies, architecture definitions
- supporting documents that are transient but are kept as part of the record of the study, such as interview notes, draft working papers and reports to management during the study.

11.2 Key deliverables

The key deliverables as permanent products are:

- *strategy statement* – (around 20-30 pages) made up of an IS strategy for the business, summary of an IT strategy for providers and management, and a description of the organisation, management and policies that will be required to make it happen. (An example structure is given at Annex D, *Example structure of an IS strategy statement*)
- *study report* – explanations, options – the audit trail of decision-making. The study report is the formal end product of the strategy study. It describes the conduct of the study and presents the findings and recommendations of the study. It constitutes an audit trail of the decisions taken, the options considered and the reasons for their selection or rejection. As well as providing full documentation for the current study, the report is a valuable contribution to the next review. The structure and contents of the study report will be agreed between the study team and the Steering Committee for the study. Topics to be covered in the study report could include:
  - the study process
  - debates on strategic themes
  - options considered and criteria for evaluation
  - findings not related to the strategy
  - working papers as annexes
  - reports of interviews as annexes (with appropriate restrictions on confidentiality).

The study report does not need to be highly detailed. Much of the material to support the contents of the report will be available in working papers and other deliverables from the study. These can be referenced from the study report. An example structure is given at Annex E, *Example of a study report*

- high level plan: how to take the strategy forward – scenarios, cost estimates, timescales for developments, the aggregate of what needs to be done; the basis of the business case. The high level plan takes you forward to the programme plans, benefits management regime, tactical plans (which could be projects, applications and/or process change) and a recommended approach for maintenance and review (for example, through benchmarking and benefits management). In the past, the plan was all about application development; today it is much wider and takes a programme-oriented view that could include organisational change and so on.

11.3 Lower level products

There are also lower level products which include:

- various working papers that will contribute to the strategy statement (their purpose is to document current thinking; see the generic list in Chapter 12, *Topics for working papers*, which should not be viewed as prescriptive)
- supporting documents that are maintained, such as statement of business assumptions
- supporting documents that are transient, such as interview notes
- annexes to the strategy statement, such as a list of policies that will need to be developed or updated.

11.4 Inputs

Some inputs will be made available to the study team at the start of the study; other inputs will be generated by them during the course of their investigations. All these inputs will be included in the project documentation.

The following information should be in existence and made available at the start of the study:

- current strategy – business plans, objectives, tactical plans (where there is no business strategy, there should be an assessment of the risks/pitfalls of not having one)
- the reasons for looking at the strategy now (these will give an indication of how radical the strategy will need to be – for example, just a routine annual review or a major change such as a merger)
- the scope (may be only a partial view at the outset) addressing a much wider view than just the IT – that is, the organisation, the business environment, boundaries and so on, and how far to go with supply/customer chains. It should include a high level statement of the potential for change and an assessment of the prior options questions; it would help in managing expectations of what will be addressed in the strategy
- current IS/IT – committed tactical plans and existing portfolio.

Other inputs that would be developed during the course of the study are:
- business assumptions
- funding: economics, financial environment
- current IS/IT: an assessment of the existing arrangements
- information requirements
- support requirements
- SWOT analysis
- study plan.

11.5 Communications

Findings from many of the products above need to be communicated to the organisation – to senior management and other stakeholders, to staff and to the user community, if appropriate.

Key messages from the strategy statement should be presented in a form that will have real impact, helping everyone concerned to understand what the changes ahead will mean for them.

Communications could be made through any or all the following:
- board papers, submissions, briefings, presentations
- staff newsletters and articles in house journals
- intranet sites with FAQs (Frequently Asked Questions)
- published guidance and information packs (see also section 5.4, *Communication Plan*).

CHAPTER TWELVE

Topics for working papers

This chapter provides an outline of the topics that could be considered during the study and shows how they would contribute to the proposed contents of the IS strategy statement. Each study is different and may require investigation of a different set of topics. For example, where the IS strategy may be particularly influenced by developments in strategic applications, business reorganisation, new technologies (such as Geographic Information Systems or Workflow systems), or policy initiatives, these could be addressed individually.

12.1 A generic set of topics

A recommended approach is to produce a working paper for each topic. Depending on the scale of the study and the complexity of the topic, working papers might be a single paragraph or several pages. Formal documentation may be very brief but will be a valuable aid in building up the strategy statement.

Documentation of the topics may be revised and recirculated during the study, as the thinking on the relevant topics develops as a result of feedback and the impact of work in other areas of the study

This list should be seen as a starting point for your own study; other topics may be added or deleted as appropriate.

A generic set of topics could include the following (the order in which they are documented will vary from study to study):
- the drivers for change
- assumptions and constraints for the IS strategy
- Organisation X: business environment
- Organisation X: business and management objectives
- review of current IS strategy
- inventory of current applications
- financing of IS/IT
- IT infrastructure and plans
- business processes and information flows
- information management
- future information systems architecture
- technological environment
- electronic document and records management
- management and technical policies for IS
- security issues
- IS opportunities and benefits in Organisation X

- IS/IT procurement and sourcing
- user support for IS/IT
- IT unit: role, responsibilities and organisation
- management of IS/IT and the strategy
- management information requirements
- IS requirements for support of policy work
- IS strategy: relationship with external organisations
- IT infrastructure: telecommunications
- IS/IT implementation plans
- strategic themes for IS in Organisation X
- IS requirements for support of business functions or units.

12.2 Outlines of the topics

- *The drivers for change* – outlines the external and internal initiatives that could affect the organisation and its business, such as new legislation.
- *Assumptions and constraints for the IS strategy review* – lists the business and other assumptions made as the basis for the conduct of the review, and which will affect the IS strategy.
- *Organisation X: business environment* – presents an overview of the current business environment of the organisation, the pressures on it which will affect the IS strategy, and the wider public sector initiatives which need to be taken into account.
- *Organisation X: business and management objectives* – summarises the objectives and priorities of the organisation, and identifies the business drivers which will affect the IS strategy.
- *Review of current IS strategy* – considers the extent to which the current IS strategy has been successful, identifies where changes are required and suggests the lessons to be learned from the progress to date.
- *Inventory of current applications* – presents summary information on the information systems and applications currently in use within the organisation, as a basis for decisions on their future within the IS strategy.
- *Financing of IS/IT* – considers the way in which IS/IT is currently financed in the organisation, including the procedures for budgeting and charging and the current levels of costs; and suggests where changes should be considered in the future.
- *IT Infrastructure and plans* – summarises the current IT infrastructure in the organisation; summarises the decisions already taken on the strategy for the IT infrastructure (the IT strategy), and identifies where additional work will be required on infrastructure definition. Identifies any issues for resolution within the IT strategy.
- *Business processes and information flows (current)* – presents a high level view of the key current business processes, information holdings within the organisation and the information flows within and outside the organisation. Summarises the current information systems architecture for the organisation.

- *Information management* – considers the way in which information is currently managed as a resource and shared within the organisation, and suggests any changes required for the future.
- *Future information systems architecture* – suggests the target IS architecture for the organisation. Identifies the processes and information flows which will be needed to support the business in the future.
- *Technological environment* – outlines the technological environment within which the IT strategy will be developed, including organisation-wide and government-wide initiatives or constraints, and developments in the industry in general which may affect the organisation. Identifies the main technological drivers and the technologies which will inform the IS and IT strategies.
- *Electronic Document and Records Management* – identifies the requirements for EDM and ERM in the organisation, taking into account any government initiatives, and suggests how these should be addressed in the IS strategy.
- *Management and technical policies for IS/IT* – identifies any existing management and technical policies for IS/IT developed by the organisation or others, and assesses the way in which they are currently operated. Suggests where any new or updated policies may be needed in the IS strategy, and the required procedures for developing and enforcing them.
- *Security issues* – identifies the security issues which need to be considered within the IS strategy, taking into account any organisation or government-wide guidance and procedures.
- *IS opportunities and benefits in Organisation X* – identifies new opportunities within the organisation for the exploitation of IS/IT to support business and management objectives. Suggests how the benefits of IS/IT can be presented and (where possible) quantified.
- *IS/IT procurement and sourcing* – assesses the current arrangements for procurement of IS/IT by the organisation, and suggests whether any changes should be made in procurement and sourcing policy and procedures.
- *User support for IS/IT* – assesses the current arrangements for supporting the user population of IS/IT facilities. Identifies requirements for user support, and suggests how these requirements should be met in the future.
- *IT unit: role, responsibilities and organisation (where appropriate)* – outlines the current role and structure of the IT unit. Considers whether any changes should be made in the responsibilities, structure or staffing of the IT unit in the light of the emerging IS strategy for the organisation.
- *Management of IS/IT and the strategy in Organisation X* – assesses the current organisational structures, roles and responsibilities in the organisation for oversight and management of IS/IT and realisation of the IS strategy (committees). Suggests any changes for the future.
  Where appropriate, includes consideration of the role of Intelligent Customer Function in the organisation.
- *Management information requirements* – identifies the requirements of organisational management for access to information, and assesses current

arrangements for provision of management information. Suggests any developments or changes required for the future.

- *IS requirements for support of policy work* – identifies the particular requirements for IS/IT support for staff involved in policy work, and how these requirements should be addressed in the IS strategy.
- *IS strategy: relationship with external organisations* – assesses the current relationship between the organisation and external organisations in respect of support for information transfer, sharing of data, interworking and so on. Suggests changes for the future.
- *IT infrastructure: telecommunications* – summarises the current arrangements for provision of telecommunications and telephony services to the organisation. Identifies any impact which future requirements and developments will have on the IT strategy.
- *IS/IT implementation plans* – suggests a high level plan of action for realising the IS/IT strategy and estimates the resource requirements for identified projects in the short term.
- *Strategic themes for IS in Organisation X* – identifies the strategic themes, which will form the core of the IS strategy, relates them to the organisation's business strategy, and outlines the developments which will be needed to progress each initiative.
- *For each business function or unit of the organisation* – IS Requirements for support of Function F [or Division D]: Identifies the particular requirements for IS/IT support of the activities of business function F and/or support of staff in Division(s) D, and how these requirements should be addressed in the IS strategy. Identifies the scope for business and process change in this area.

12.3 Inputs to the strategy statement

Figure 5 shows where each of these topics feeds into the strategy statement.

Figure 5: *Working papers contributing to IS strategy statement*	**Statement of IS strategy**	**Working papers contributing to statement**
	1 INTRODUCTION	
	1.1 Purpose of the IS strategy	
	1.2 Benefits of the IS strategy	IS opportunities and benefits
	1.3 Status of the IS strategy	Review of current IS strategy
	1.4 Scope of the strategy	IS strategy: relationship with external organisations
	1.5 IS strategy and business planning	Management of IS/IT and strategy
	1.6 Purpose of the IS strategy statement	
	1.7 Structure of the statement	
	2 STRATEGY STATEMENT	
	2.1 Business environment and business direction	Drivers for change Assumptions and constraints for the IS strategy

		Organisation X: business environment
		Organisation X: business and management objectives
2.2	Information requirements of the organisation	Inventory of current applications
		Business processes and information flows
		Information management
		Management information requirements
		IS for support of policy work
2.3	Current IS/IT in the organisation	Review of current IS strategy
		Inventory of current applications
2.4	Information systems strategy and IS vision for the organisation	Electronic document and records management
		IS opportunities and benefits
		Management information requirements
		IS for support of policy work
		IS requirements for support of business functions and units
2.5	Key applications; application and data architecture	Future information systems architecture
		IS opportunities and benefits
		IS for support of policy work
		IS requirements for support of business functions and units
2.6	IT (technical) strategy, technical architecture	IT infrastructure and plans
		Technological environment
		IT infrastructure: telecommunications
2.7	Organisation, management and policies for IS/IT	Financing of IS/IT
		Management and technical policies for IS/IT
		Security issues
		IS/IT procurement and sourcing
		User support for IS/IT
		IT unit: roles, responsibilities and organisation
		Management of IS/IT and the strategy
		IS strategy: relationship with external organisations
3	REALISATION OF THE STRATEGY	
3.1	Strategic themes for IS	Strategic themes for IS
3.2	Candidates for action	IS/IT implementation plans
3.3	High level plans: selected portfolio, plans and developments	Financing of IS/IT
		IS opportunities and benefits
		IS/IT implementation plans
	ANNEXES – additional material	As appropriate; backup details from working papers

Annexes

Management and technical policies

Policies can be regarded as either 'enabling' or 'restraining'. Enabling policies are those which aim to support, promote and encourage the deployment of effective information systems and services. Restraining policies are those which aim to control or constrain the IS activities in the various parts of the organisation, either for their own good or for the greater good of the organisation as a whole.

Examples of areas where the organisation may need to introduce enabling policies are:
- central provision and allocation of IS resources, such as equipment, technical staff, software and services
- arrangements with suppliers, procurement procedures and contractual terms
- the role of providers in the provision of support and training, and user documentation
- the provision of common services, such as generic application systems to meet common requirements, to all parts of the organisation
- procedures for prioritisation of developments, the planning of a phased introduction of facilities to the organisation, and the implementation of pilot projects where relevant
- the use of external services, such as consultants, database services and maintenance services
- policies for provision and monitoring of ergonomic aspects of IT systems, including the user interface
- procedures for system implementation and project management, such as use of the PRINCE methodology.

Examples of areas where the organisation may need to introduce restraining policies are:
- requirements for compatibility and conformance with standards and guidelines on selection and use of software and document formats
- definition of procedures for disaster recovery, system security and systems audit
- standards and procedures for identifying, validating, storing and accessing shared information at work-group, business function or corporate level
- operating procedures for users of desktop facilities, including policies on local purchase and import of software, and exchange of data media
- procedures for on-line and off-line document storage, naming, retention, purging and archiving.

Business case development

This annex summarises the development of the business case for external procurements, especially PFI projects. It is not generically applicable to all candidates for action.

Strategic Outline Case (SOC)

Phase 1: Initial scoping

The primary purpose of this phase is:

a to establish business need and strategic fit

b to indicate the way forward in terms of a preferred option.

Structure and content

Executive summary
Document structure.

The Strategic Case

Investment Objectives
Project objectives and return on investment.

Strategic context

Organisational overview
Snapshot of the purpose of the organisation and organisational structure.

Business strategy and objectives
Existing and future business plans, including customer base and market for services.

IS/IT strategy and objectives

Existing and future plans for underpinning IS/IT.

Outline Business Case (OBC)

Phase 2: Detailed planning

Before OJEC, the primary purpose of this phase is:

a to validate the preferred way forward

b to assess potential VFM, affordability and achievablity.

Structure and content

Executive summary
Document structure.

The Strategic Case

Update and full coverage of SOC
Investment objectives ranked and made SMART (Specific, Measurable, Achieveable, Relevant, Timed).

Strategic context

Organisational overview
Revisit earlier assumptions, including changes within external environment.

Business strategy and objectives
Update as required.

IS/IT strategy and objectives

Update as required.

Full Business Case (FBC)

Phase 3: Selection of solution

Following competition, the primary purpose of this phase is to select the service solution which optimises VFM, within the overall constraints of affordabilty and achievability.

Structure and content

Executive summary
Document structure.

The Strategic Case

Overview of the strategic context, including objectives of the organisation and the project; and review of assumptions underlying the strategic analysis and effects of any changes since the OBC.

Strategic context

Organisational overview
Revisit earlier assumptions, including changes within external environment.

Business strategy and objectives
Update as required.

IS/IT strategy and objectives

Update as required.

Strategic Outline Case (SOC)

Strategic need
Existing arrangements (if any).

Business needs – current and future.

Potential scope and service requirements
Description of required business outcomes and high level service requirements.

The Economic Case
Main business options
(SWOT analysis) – main variants, both in terms of scope and service delivery, including 'do nothing' or 'do minimum' options.

Preferred business option
identified by initial assessment of potential benefits and 'fit' with investment objectives.

Outline Business Case (OBC)

Strategic need
Update as required.

Update as required.

Desired scope and service requirements
Detailed description of business outcomes and high level service requirement.

Procurement strategy
- use of PSC (Public Sector Comparator)
- EC/GATT regulations
- evaluation criteria
- selection of preferred bidder.

The Economic Case
Main business options
Revisit earlier options against a SMART/ ranked investment objectives b benefits criteria (top 10 weighted).

Preferred business option
Review of assumptions underlying the SOC to demonstrate how any changes have affected the ranking of options, including benefits.

Full Business Case (FBC)

Strategic need
Update as required.

Update as required.

Scope and service requirements
Update as required.

The procurement process
- description of process
- OJEC Notice (attachment)
- summary of ITN (Invitation to Negotiate)
- prequalification, long and short listing
- use of advisers.

The Economic Case
Main business options
Summary of the OBC, including description of long and short list of options considered and results of economic appraisals, benefits analysis, financial analysis and sensitivity analysis.

Preferred business option
Review of assumptions underlying the SOC to demonstrate how any changes have affected the ranking of options, including benefits.

Potential investment (funding) options
Including privately (PFI) and publicly financed.

Preferred option
Including description of benefits and risk initial assessment of supply-side capability and likely affordability.

Potential investment (funding) options
Develop the reference project or public sector comparator (PSC) through market soundings etc. (to test for affordability).

Preferred option
Evaluate against the case for PFI, in terms of potential VFM. Outcome of above analysis.

Sensitivity analysis
Description of main variables.

Benefits (by key categories):
a type – task, operational, strategic
b timescale – short, medium, long-term
c value – high, medium, low
d quantitative (£)/qualitatiative
e direct, indirect.

Potential investment (funding) options
Full description, including explanation of any updates that have been made to place the PSC on the same footing as the PFI solution.

Preferred option
i Reasons for selection of preferred bidder (if appropriate)
ii Result of:
a economic appraisal VFM analysis Risk adjusted NPV comparison of the PSC and PFI option(s); and (if necessary) EAC of options. Full description of costs and benefits attached to Economic Appraisals
b evaluation of non-quantifiable benefits.

Sensitivity analysis
Description of main variables.

Benefits
- full description of benefits (both quantitative and qualitative; direct and indirect)
- full indication of differences in the level of benefits delivered under the PSC and PFI options.

Strategic Outline Case (SOC)

Recommended way forward.

Outline Business Case (OBC)

Business and PFI service risks

Full assessment of the cost of risks retained under the PSC by DBFO category (Must be included in the Economic Appraisal for PSC in accordance with Treasury Taskforce and 'Green Book' guidance).

The Commercial Case

Outline of potential service arrangement
- risk transfer
- payment mechanism
- personnel (inc TUPE) implications
- preferred contract length
- proposed key contractual clauses
- implementation timescale.

The Financial Case

Revenue implications of PSC option against:
a 3 year Treasury Expenditure Plan
b Dept/Agency I&E account
c Balance sheet
d Cash flow (as required).

Financial appraisals, if required, including description of assumptions.

Full Business Case (FBC)

Business and PFI service risks

Agreed risk allocation matrix
Key service risks, including method of measurement
NPV analysis of risks retained under each option
Non-quantifiable risks (weighting and scoring matrix).

The Commercial Case

The preferred PFI solution
- description of Service Provider/Consortium
- full description of PFI Solution (see below).

TU involvement/TUPE etc
Summary of contract structure
Agreed delivery timetable.

The Financial Case

Revenue implications of PFI and PSC options against:
a 3 year Treasury Expenditure Plan
b Dept/Agency I&E account
c Balance sheet
d Cash flow (as required).

Financial appraisals, if required, including description of assumptions.

Likely accounting (FRS5)Treatment

Project management arrangements
Project roles and responsibilities
Project plan
Use of advisers.

Economic appraisals
a PSC (including benefits and risk adjustment)
b 'Do nothing'/'do minimum' option (including risk adjustment)
c Sensitivity analysis (of main cost, benefits and timing for each option).

Financial appraisals
As required.

Accounting (FRS5) treatment

Project management arrangements
Contract management arrangements
Risk management strategy
Benefits realisation plan
PIR/PER arrangements
Contingency plans.

Economic appraisals
a PFI service solution (including benefits and risk adjustment)
b PSC (including benefits and risk adjustment)
c 'Do nothing'/'do minimum' option (including risk adjustment)
d Sensitivity analysis (of main cost, benefits and timing for each option).

Financial appraisals
As required.

Document specification format

This annex provides a suggested format for document specification as an aid to quality review.

Organisation X: IS strategy review document specification

Title: _____ *Document ref:* _____

Author: _____ *Specification issue no:* _____

Document due date (final): _____ *Specification issue date:* _____

Background to the document, reason for producing it; place of the document within the project and documentation set; relationship to other documents in the review:

_____

_____

_____

_____

_____

Objectives of the document; what its production is intended to achieve:

_____

_____

_____

_____

_____

_____

Scope of the document; questions and issues to be addressed; constraints; exclusions:

_____

_____

_____

_____

_____

Inputs to production of the document; sources of information; other documents and working papers to be considered as inputs:

_____

_____

_____

_____

_____

Notes: distribution of the document:

_____

_____

_____

_____

_____

Example structure of an IS strategy statement

This annex provides an example structure of an IS strategy statement, which should be tailored to individual circumstances.

1 *Introduction*
1.1 Purpose of the IS strategy
1.2 Benefits of the IS strategy
1.3 Status of the IS strategy
1.4 Scope of the IS strategy
1.5 IS strategy and business planning
1.6 Purpose of the IS strategy statement
1.7 Structure of the statement

2 *Strategy statement*
2.1 Business environment and business direction
2.2 Information requirements of the organisation
2.3 Current IS/IT in the organisation
2.4 IS strategy and IS vision for the organisation
2.5 Key applications, applications/data architecture
2.6 IT (technical) strategy and IT architecture
2.7 Organisation, management and policies for IS/IT

3 *Realisation of the strategy*
3.1 Strategic themes for IS – their description
3.2 Selected portfolio candidates for action:
3.3 High level plans

Annexes will contain detailed material on particular topics – for example:
- summary of business process analysis
- summary of information requirements analysis
- summary of current information systems inventory
- summary of proposed information system architecture
- summary of proposed technical architecture
- details of proposed implementation plans, key developments and outline costings
- details of business case for the strategy, and benefits to be achieved from realisation
- summary of IS/IT policies required
- functions and Terms of Reference for organisational units involved in the realisation of the strategy
- summary of relevant new technologies.

Example structure of study report

This annex provides an example structure of the study report, to be adapted as required. Sections of the study report might cover:

Background to the strategy study:
- why the study was commissioned
- progress made since last strategy study or review
- organisation and environment: summary of current issues
- organisation and business background
- business direction and constraints.

IS/IT environment:
- summary of previous IS strategy
- status of current IS
- major current information systems and developments in hand
- summary of IT and infrastructure
- current organisation for management of IS/IT
- organisation for demand and supply sides.

Structure of the study:
- Terms of Reference for the study/review
- composition and Terms of Reference of the Steering Committee
- study team: full- and part-time members
- use of consultants
- timescales and resources
- study plan.

Conduct of the study:
- phases of the study
- milestones and checkpoints in the study
- key activities
- interviews conducted
- workshops held
- deliverables produced
- quality management in the study
- difficulties encountered and lessons learned.

Options and choices:
- reasons for recommended strategy
- evaluation criteria used in the study

- how issues were identified
- how the themes were chosen
- what shaped the selection of the strategy
- consideration of scenarios for realisation of the strategy
- ideas to carry forward.

Further information

Companion CCTA guides

- IS Management Guides
  - *Strategic Management of Information Systems*
  - *Managing Change*
  - *Managing Performance*
  - *Managing Services*
  - *Acquisition*
  - *Techniques*
  - *The Informed Partner*
- *Managing Successful Programmes*
- The IT Infrastructure Library (ITIL)

Further reading/ sources

These include:

- *Strategic Management and Planning in the Public Sector*
  Robert J Smith
  Longman 1994; ISBN 0-582-23892-7

- *Strategic Planning for Public and Non-profit Organisations*
  John M Bryson
  Jossey-Bass 1995; ISBN 1-55542-087-7

- *Strategic Management of Public and Third Sector Organisations*
  Paul C Nutt and Robert W Backoff
  Jossey-Bass 1992; ISBN 1-55542-386-8

- *An Organisational Approach to IS Strategy-making in Information Management*
  (M J Earl, ed.); OUP 1996; ISBN 0-19-825760-0

- *Strategic Planning for Information Systems*
  J Ward and P Griffiths
  John Wiley & Sons 1996, ISBN 0-471-96183-3

- *Strategic Management for the Public Services*
  Paul Joyce
  Open University Press 1999, ISBN 0-335-20047-8

The CCTA website

For more information on CCTA's ongoing work in developing best practice, visit the CCTA website at *www.ccta.gov.uk*

Index